THINK A$TROLOGY & GROW RICH!

SUCCESS FORMULAS
BUSINESS, CAREER
& INVESTMENT
DECISION-MAKING

PAUL B FARRELL, MRP, JD, PhD

THINK A$TROLOGY & GROW RICH
with
The New Money A$trology
Success Formulas
for Business, Career & Investment
Decision-Making

by Paul B. Farrell, J.D., Ph.D.

Copyright 2018 by Paul B. Farrell
"25th Anniversary Edition" 2018
Original Copyright 1993 by Paul B. Farrell
First Printing 1993
Printed in the United States of America
ISBN 978-0963884718
ISBN 0963884719

All rights are reserved. No part of this book may be reproduced of transmitted in any form or by any means, electronic or mechanical, including photocopying, recording or by any information storage and retrieval system without written permission from the author, except for the inclusion of brief quotations in a review.

Library of Congress Cataloging in Publication Data
Farrell, Paul B.
THINK A$TROLOGY & GROW RICH
Paul B. Farrell - 1st Edition
Bibliography
Includes index.
1. Business & Economic Forecasting
2. Success Motivation
3. Astrological Sciences

Lib. Cong. Card Cat. #93-93654

"The Past Does
Not Predict The Future"

Anthony Robbins

"The Future Is But
A Repetition of The Past"

W. D. Gann

"No Past, No Future,
Only The Eternal Now."

Lao Tsu

TABLE of CONTENTS

DEDICATION TO NAPOLEON HILL	i
CAN ASTROLOGY REALLY HELP YOU MAKE MONEY? A SPECIAL NOTE TO THE SKEPTIC	1
MONEY A$TROLOGY 101 - A PRIMER	3

PART ONE: THE "PARADIGM SHIFT" TO A NEW ASTROLOGY

THE 5 FORCES CREATING A NEW ASTROLOGY   9

Force 1. **WALL STREET MONEY** - J. P. Morgan & W. D. Gann   13
Force 2. **MODERN PSYCHOLOGY** - Carl G. Jung   19
Force 3. **SCIENCE & TECHNOLOGY** - Michel Gauquelin   25
Force 4. **HI-TECH MYTHOLOGY** - Joseph Campbell & George Lucas   31
Force 5. **CREATIVE ACTION** - Roger von Oech   35

PART TWO: HOW THE NEW ASTROLOGY WORKS

THE 7 RULES OF SUCCESSFUL DECISION-MAKING   41

RULE 1. **TARGETING THE RIGHT MISSION & GOALS**   45
RULE 2. **THE RIGHT TIMING FOR YOUR ACTIONS**   59
RULE 3. **PREDICTING YOUR COMPETITION'S DECISIONS**   69
RULE 4. **LEVERAGING THE RIGHT PARTNERS & TEAM**   81
RULE 5. **PICKING THE RIGHT LOCATIONS & MARKETS**   86
RULE 6. **RISK MANAGEMENT & SECOND OPINIONS**   89
RULE 7. **THE POWER OF TOTAL COMMITMENT**   95

PART THREE: APPENDICES

EPILOGUE: A NEW ASTROLOGY FOR THE 21st CENTURY   101

1. RESOURCES & READINGS   103

2. CHECKLIST: HOW TO SELECT AN ASTROLOGER   107

3. CRISIS SURVIVAL KIT FOR EMERGENCIES   110

4. BASIC TOOLS FOR ASTROLOGICAL ANALYSIS   113
    . **MINI-CRASH COURSE IN ASTROLOGY**   114
    . **AN ASTROLOGICAL PROFILE ANALYSIS**   115
    . **10 PERSONALITY PROFILES FOR SUCCESS**   116
    . **ASTROLOGICAL "ZIP-CODE" INTERPRETATIONS**   118

DEDICATION

NAPOLEON HILL, THE ULTIMATE ENTREPRENEUR

"Whatever the mind of man can conceive and believe, it can achieve," Napoleon Hill in *Think and Grow Rich*.

Napoleon Hill was one of the truly great teachers of all time. Napoleon Hill's *Science Of Success* inspired more entrepreneurs and created more millionaires than any other single person in this century.

For decades he has been a role-model for virtually every other successful motivational leader in America, from Anthony Robbins, Wayne Dyer and Charles Garfield, to Denis Waitley, Earl Nightingale and Zig Ziglar. In fact, the title of Robbins' book, *Awaken The Giant Within*, is virtually identical to one of the chapter headings of an earlier book Hill co-authored with Clement Stone, *Success Through A Positive Mental Attitude*.

Although Hill's genius was focused on success, money and financial power, in a strange way, at times some of his writings echo a strong sense of social consciousness, for the riches he speaks of are, in the final analysis, riches of the spirit (perhaps reflecting the fact that he wrote *Think and Grow Rich* while on Roosevelt's New Deal staff during the 1930's).

His odd mixture of economics and spirituality was underscored throughout *Success Through A Positive Mental Attitude*, where Hill and Stone bottom-lined this message; "for many years [we taught] the 17 success principles. The title of the course was *PMA, The Science of Success*." These 17 success principles:

1. *Positive Mental Attitude*
2. *Definiteness of purpose*
3. *Going the extra mile*
4. *Accurate thinking*
5. *Self-discipline*
6. *The master mind*
7. *Applied faith*
8. *A pleasing personality*
9. *Personal initiative*
10. *Enthusiasm*
11. *Controlled attention*
12. *Teamwork*
13. *Learning from defeat*
14. *Creative vision*
15. *Budgeting time & money*
16. *Sound physical & mental health*
17. *Using the cosmic force*

Although they had a total of 17 principles, Hill and Stone emphasized over and over that a Positive Mental Attitude (PMA) was the key principle to creating a successful life.

THE "SHORT CUT" TO SUCCESS ... A POSITIVE MENTAL ATTITUDE

In one chapter, right after listing the 17 success principles, Hill and Stone give us their *bottom-line* secret:

"We want to show you the short cut to riches. We want you to take the direct route. Now to take the direct route, you must necessarily think with PMA ... if you really think with PMA, you will automatically follow through with action ... Therefore, the short cut to riches for you ... *Think with PMA and Grow Rich!*"

Positive Mental Attitude is also the essential bottom-line in the new astrology for the 21st Century. On one hand, this new astrology is inspirational, a tool empowering you to achieve your highest potentials in your business and personal life. Equally important, it is practical, a tool helping you make better decisions about money, career, business, finances and investments.

So it is with a delicate balance of humility and chutzpah that I dedicate this book to Napoleon Hill, the great entrepreneur and teacher who inspired me to *Think A$trology and Grow Rich!*

CAN ASTROLOGY HELP YOU MAKE MONEY? READ THIS ... IF YOU'RE SKEPTICAL.

A PERSONAL NOTE TO ENTREPRENEURS, TRADERS, INVESTORS & EXECUTIVES IN BUSINESS & FINANCE

THE "BEST KEPT SECRET" on WALL STREET & CORPORATE AMERICA!

If you're skeptical about whether astrology can help you make decisions about money, I don't blame you. I still am. In fact, I hope you'll *always* have a healthy skepticism about astrology ... as well as any other method of predicting the future, whether invented by economists, politicians, journalists, theologians or anyone else. I question astrology all the time. But it works.

My first exposure to astrology came in 1975 while I was a vice president with Morgan Stanley & Company, the international investment banking firm founded by J. P. Morgan. An ad executive friend took me to one of Joseph Campbell's "Mythological Meditation" workshops, covering mythology, Jungian psychology, astrology, mysticism, shamanism, the tarot and I Ching. It was almost a year before I reluctantly made an appointment with my first astrologer. Sure, I was curious, but I still felt stupid about "this *Ladies Home Journal* stuff."

Today I laugh at myself for thinking that I was "cheating on the firm," only to discover later that old J. P. Morgan himself, and many others on Wall Street and in Corporate America, had beaten me to it. While I was executive vice president of the Financial News Network, the national business news channel, I began seeing even more of the growing power of astrology.

> **THE SILENT CONSPIRACY ON THE LEADING EDGE OF A REVOLUTION**
> "A lot of top guys use astrology, but they don't admit it," says Arch Crawford, known as the Wall Street Astrologer, "People don't want to be thought of as fools." Crawford is a former Merrill Lynch market analyst and, since 1977, the publisher of a successful investment advisory newsletter using astrology. One of his clients demanded delivery of the newsletter in a plain brown wrapper.

Such is the fear surrounding the possibility of using astrology to predict the future, a backlash that was obvious in the flap about President Reagan's astrologer; notable in the extraordinary seventeen pages of coverage in *Time* magazine. Astrology went underground. Today most men and women on Wall Street and Corporate America treat their trips to astrologers private and confidential - *like visits to their physicians, attorneys, accountants, therapists and priests.* Why invite trouble. Who needs the aggravation. The information *is* personal, and the meetings are none of anybody's darn business.

WHY ARE 27,500,000 *WORKING* AMERICANS USING ASTROLOGY!?

Like many revolutions, this one is growing rapidly but quietly, underground and behind the scenes. You could easily miss the initial opportunities. So maybe it's time you should start to *think astrology and grow rich.* When you do, you'll certainly be in excellent company, and on the leading edge of one of the major new developments of the late 20th Century.

Questions about money and careers, financial deals, business profits and economic prosperity probably drive more people to astrologers than romance, health and spiritual enlightenment.

Decades ago, J. P. Morgan's belief in astrology was so strong that he once remarked, "millionaires don't hire astrologers, billionaires do!"

Morgan's astrologer, Evangeline Adams, was advising not only the billionaire financier, but also three successive Presidents of the New York Stock Exchange, as well as James J. Hill, the founder of the American railroad system, and many other world leaders in banking, commerce and industry. Adams clients also included celebrities such as the opera singer, Enrico Caruso and William Jennings Bryan, the great attorney.

About the same time Morgan was building his fortune, W. D. Gann, a mathematician and astrologer was trading in the commodities markets. His trading techniques not only netted him a personal fortune of $50 million in his lifetime, his methods are the basis of the "technical analysis" systems used by most stock brokers today. Moreover, one successful astrologer claims that President Reagan's Treasury Secretary, Donald Regan, once quoted the statistic that, in fact, 47% of today's Wall Street brokers use astrologers.

A QUIET REVOLUTION CREATING A NEW "ASTROLOGY OF SUCCESS!"

Fortunately, astrological advice is now available to a much broader audience than Wall Street and the *Forbes* magazine list of 400 billionaires. For today, money is still the hot topic it was when Adams wrote that, "fully one third of the people who came to see me from distant points ask me how they can seek their fortunes in the stock market."

SUCCESS TOOL: SOME MONEY-MAKING DEMOGRAPHICS

Time magazine, in reviewing former White House Chief of Staff Donald Regan's book, *For The Record,* estimated that 50,000,000 Americans rely on astrology for direction. A French Institute of Public Opinion poll went further; 43% of their population "believe that astrology is a true science." And a 1990 United States research study by Gallup Pollsters estimated that 25% of Americans already use astrology in a variety of decisions.

Based on our national labor pool of 110,000,000 people, we can estimate that at least 27,500,000 *working* Americans are using astrology. That's a powerful network of believers. And at an average annual income of $20,000, you have over $500,000,000,000 of economic power. *You can't afford to ignore astrology!*

The power of astrology was quite obvious to me as an associate editor of the *Los Angeles Herald Examiner* newspaper. More disgruntled readers would call in to complain when we moved the astrology column than any other time!

The bottom-line is that throughout history, astrology has played a major role in the decisions of many key players on Wall Street and Corporate America, as well as millions of other Americans concerned about economic issues. All too often the answers provided by the economists and other business forecasters just aren't good enough.

Successful decision-makers want a competitive *edge,* so they turn to astrology for everything from planning new careers, getting loans and forecasting the market, to predicting the success of new ventures, business partnerships and real estate investment opportunities.

For these millions, astrology works!

The answer is ... Yes, astrology can help you make money, too.

MONEY A$TROLOGY 101 - A PRIMER
10 WAYS BUSINESS & FINANCIAL EXECUTIVES, INVESTORS, SECURITIES TRADERS & ENTREPRENEURS USE ASTROLOGY TODAY

Astrology is quietly finding its way into all areas of the business and financial worlds. The revolution Tom Peters talks about in *Thriving on Chaos* and his other books has brought with it the downsizing of many large and small corporations, and is forcing many talented people to shift into new careers, or go into business for themselves and become entrepreneurs.

In today's unstable economic climate, many men and women are finding themselves at major turning points in their lives, reexamining existing careers and businesses, ready to start new lives in the rapidly changing business world.

Today's astrologers can help you make key decisions, seize opportunities and go for it! In this dynamic world, you must be aware of several important ways that astrology can help in the future, ways to increase your profits as your new career or business becomes an ongoing venture.

> **MONEY TIP:** As you read through the following list of the 10 ways astrology is *already* being used in the business and financial world, I want you to think of how you can use each one of these techniques to capitalize a new business, or expand into a new market or product line, or invest in a new project, or joint venture a real estate deal, or as a tool in any other profit-making opportunity.

Here's my basic primer on the key techniques and applications of the emerging new Money Astrology. Significantly, *all* of these are already in practical use by various professionals and executives in the business and financial world. Many of them are *already in widespread use.*

You can also profit using these same techniques, which will be discussed more thoroughly in later chapters. Here I just want you to get a feel of some potential uses of astrology in *your* business life:

1. PICKING A START DATE FOR YOUR NEW VENTURE.

Often business owners use a tool called *electional* astrology, to pick the best "birth time" to start a new business. In effect, you get to pick the time the new "baby" is going to be born, and increase it's potential for success in the business world. You can use the same technique to incorporate a business, or re-incorporate an existing one, or kick off a new marketing campaign, or any other new venture. It works. *(also see rule 6 in part two)*

2. SETTING YOUR BUSINESS OBJECTIVES.

Anyone starting a new business *must* have a clear mission statement, setting specific goals for you and your organization. Otherwise, it's aimless, like a missile without a target. An analysis of the charts of the founders and key officers, as well as the chart of the business itself, may be used in combination with other techniques, to give the business some direction in planning its marketing, finances and strategic goals. *(see rules 1 & 2)*

3. SELECTING THE BEST TEAM & PARTNERS FOR YOU.

For centuries, astrological compatibility studies have been used to analyze the success potentials and limitations of partners in personal relationships and marriages. Today, businesses are using these astrological compatibility studies to select executives for business partnerships and structure corporate executive teams, creating optimum business "marriages." *(see part two, rule 4)*

4. HIRING YOUR STAFF & PLANNING CAREERS.

Many individuals already use astrologers to help pick jobs or plan careers. Today's business organizations are becoming clients, using astrologers to screen and fit potential employees to specific job specifications, along with psychological tests. In the last few decades this work has been aided by some rather innovative scientific studies correlating the birthcharts of thousands of successful men and women. These studies are now available in evaluating the success potentials of individual applicants for key positions. *(see rules 1 & 4)*

5. ANALYZING YOUR CONTRACTS & AGREEMENTS.

The technique of electional astrology is also being used in selecting the right times and dates to sign contracts. In addition, members of the business and financial community often use astrologers to analyze existing agreements already signed, such as a real estate sales contracts. They cast charts based on the time a deal is signed, and evaluate the probabilities of a favorable closing. The horary technique is another astrological tool used for predicting success. With horary, questions are poised about any business and financial decisions, charts cast for the specific moment in time the question is asked, and the answers used as aids in making decisions. *(see rule 6)*

6. BUDGETING YOUR PROFITS & LOSSES.

Creative astrological techniques are also used to compare the natal charts and transits of business organizations and their key executives, along with other external cycles in nature. These forecasts of the ups and downs in business fortunes can be used as additional input in estimating profit expectations and capital allocations. *(see rule 3)*

7. LOCATING YOUR BEST MARKET NICHE.

In recent years a number of techniques have been developed to help analyze the astrological impact of new geographic location. Astro*Carto*Graphy is one of these tools discussed below. Although an individual's or organization's relocation chart will remain similar to their natal chart, the house positions and current transits may be more or less favorable in a new geographic location. This can significantly increase or decrease opportunities for your business or career. This astrological technique can be used combined with horary and electional techniques to assist in making new plant and new market decisions for businesses, or test a job offer or promotion involving a new location. *(rule 5)*

8. ANALYZING SPECIFIC STOCK PRICES.

Some analysts cast charts based on the date of incorporation of a company, and make their predictions on stock prices from the current planetary transits and other factors. In addition, many financial professionals now use astrology, along with technical analysis, to track turning points in the prices of publicly traded corporations and commodities. The form of technical analysis commonly used in the stock markets today was originally developed decades ago by a astrologer-mathematician who began tracking fluctuations in commodity prices using planetary transits. He became a millionaire and his methods are still in wide use on Wall Street today. *(see rule 3)*

9. FORECASTING THE FINANCIAL MARKETS.

Financial astrologers also use a wide range of astrological and other natural cycles to forecast trends on the overall stock and commodities markets. Some use the charts of the New York Stock Exchange, the United States and those of other countries. In addition, cyclical changes in sun spots and lunar nodes, as well as the major aspects of the transiting planets, aid forecasters in predicting probable *buy/sell* days for the stock market as a whole. You should know how sensitive your business is to fluctuations in the overall markets. *(see rule 3)*

10. PREDICTING GENERAL ECONOMIC TRENDS.

Not surprisingly, there are also economic and political gurus who rely, at least in part, on astrological as well as other natural cycles in making predictions about the national economy. At this level of thinking, astrological insights merge with geo-political and metaphysical intuitions, as well as economics, statistics and the computer sciences, as a basis of forecasting the future. Often, the astrologer's solutions are the most perceptive and accurate! *(see rule 3)*

MONEY A$TROLOGY IS AN INNOVATIVE NEW SUCCESS TOOL

Today's volatile business environment has set the stage for a radical economic transformation. More than at any time in history, there are powerful forces demanding new solutions to the problems of our nation and the planet.

For centuries, the astrological arts and sciences have been an essential tool in the business and political decision-making of other societies, such as the Japanese and Arabian cultures. Anwar Sadat once said to a friend, *"We believe in astrology as you Americans believe in religion. It is a science that gives us the edge in decision-making ... and a guide through the storm."*

Today, the Wall Street and Corporate America, along with other segments of our culture are shifting away from a rigid, left-brain, rational approach that has dominated our thinking for the last three centuries since the Newtonian revolution. Witness the recent business books, *Thriving on Chaos, The Tao Jones Averages, Virtual Reality* and *A Whack On The Side Of The Head*.

As this shift accelerates during this last decade of the millennium, we can expect more and more American business and financial leaders will be exploring the creative uses of the astrological sciences, as they search for alternative perspectives in dealing with the unpredictable future, so they can better forecast, plan and decide on their future strategies!

THE BOTTOM-LINE ON THE NEW MONEY A$TROLOGY 101
If you want to expand as an entrepreneur and start a new business or develop an existing business, or if you're trading securities, or investing in a new project or partnership, or if you are considering a new career, you should seriously examine these astrological techniques. *They are already in broad use in today's competitive business and financial world ... even though very few executives and financial advisors will publicly admit it.* With these astrological tools, you can minimize your risks while generating profitable new opportunities!

MILESTONES IN THE EMERGING NEW "MONEY A$TROLOGY"

1875 — SAMUEL BENNER publishes *Benner's Prophecies of Future Ups & Downs in Prices*, the first book published based on economic research and forecasting of trends and cycles in the business world.

1895 — GUSTAVE LE BON'S classic on mass psychology, *The Crowd: A Study Of The Popular Mind*, influences market thinking, paving the way for the development of today's "technical analysis" methods.

1900 — J.P. MORGAN makes his famous statement, "Millionaires don't hire astrologers, billionaires do!" A dramatic start for the paradigm shift.

1902 — W.D. GANN, an astrologer & mathematician credited with creating "technical analysis," begins his professional career trading in the commodities markets, and before 1950 he also creates a fortune of $50,000,000 with his new market technology.

1908 — DR. CARL JUNG'S scientific research reports 97% accuracy in using astrology as diagnostic technique in analyzing personality problems.

1926 — Russian economist, N.D. KONDRATIEFF, publishes his classic paper on "long waves" or oscillations in international economic activities.

1930 — DR. CARL JUNG challenges astrologers to become more scientific.

1932 — J.P. MORGAN'S astrologer, EVANGELINE ADAMS, writes that she was advising three Presidents of the New York Stock Exchange, and many other leaders of the American business and financial world.

1941 — EDWARD DEWEY, former Chief Economist, U.S. Department of Commerce, creates the prestigious Foundation for the Study of Cycles, later referred to in NAPOLEON HILL and CLEMENT STONE'S *Success Through Mental Positive Attitude* as a powerful resource in the successes of many business men and women.

1950 — DR. MICHEL GAUQUELIN, statistician, psychologist and astrologer, begins 40 years of scientific correlation studies on the birth data of 500,000 successful men and women in many fields, including, politicians, athletes, scientists, surgeons, artists, writers, musicians, military leaders and others in positions of power and authority.

1959 — DAVID WILLIAMS publishes *Astro-Economics* and *Business Cycles Forecasting*; his classic, *Financial Astrology* is published later.

1971 — EDWARD DEWEY and OG MANDINO, editor of *Success* magazine, publish their classics: *Cycles, the Mysterious Forces That Trigger Events*, and *The Science of Prediction*, summarizing the first three decades of research at the Foundation for the Study of Cycles.

1975+ — ROBERT HAND, STEPHEN ARROYO and other psychologists publish major texts on astrological cycles and personality. TYL, POTTENGER, BINDER, RATHGEB, GREEN & other professionals write key texts on psychological and vocational astrology, building on the new focus on scientific research and computer technology initiated by Gauquelin.

1977 — ARCH CRAWFORD, a former Merrill Lynch market analyst known as "The Wall Street Astrologer," begins publishing his market newsletter, *Crawford Perspectives*, one of the first on stock market astrology.

1980+ — LARRY PESAVENTO, commodities trader begins publishing his monthly newsletter, *AstroCycles*, and three financial books, including *Planetary Harmonics of Speculative Markets*. Others active in market research, including MASON SEXTON, CAROL MULL, JEANNE LONG; BILL MERIDIAN develops AstroAnalyst software with ROBERT HAND; HENRY WEINGARTEN creates The Astrologers Fund, an investment vehicle. The World Conference on Astro-Economics is organized.

PART ONE
THE PARADIGM SHIFT

FIVE POWERFUL FORCES CREATING A NEW A$TROLOGY FOR THE 21st CENTURY

PART ONE: THE PARADIGM SHIFT
FIVE POWERFUL FORCES CREATING A NEW ASTROLOGY FOR THE 21st CENTURY

WHY DOES ASTROLOGY WORK? AND WHY IS IT CHANGING?

Astrology has been used as a forecasting tool since 4,000 B.C. However, the *technology* of professional astrologers remained fairly constant for 6,000 years, until the beginning of the 20th Century A.D.

Astrology grew up as part of the science and function of astronomers who advised the leaders of church and state, and their success depended on their accuracy in the art of forecasting the future. Astrologers ventured into everything political and economic, medical and psychological, but the system changed very little over a long time, practiced more as an intuitive art than a science.

THE PARADIGM SHIFT: FROM CHAOS TO A "NEW WORLD ORDER"

We are now in a major paradigm shift, the great quantum leap of 20th century science and technology, with its impact on psychology, the global economy and so much more. The last one occurred with the Newtonian Revolution 300 years ago. And with it comes many new opportunities for men and women in businesses, investing and entrepreneurial ventures.

> **WHAT IS A "PARADIGM" AND WHY IS THE DARN THING "SHIFTING?"**
> The scientist and historian Thomas Kuhn defined a paradigm as a worldview held by an entire community, nation or even a civilization, not merely an individual or personal way of thinking. For over three hundred years our culture has been guided by the Newtonian mechanistic belief in a clockworks universe. Kuhn's 1969 classic, *The Structure of Scientific Revolutions*, gave focus to the fundamental shift occurring throughout our world.
> Kuhn observes in classic "that any science is, at any given moment in history, a prisoner of fundamental prejudices which he called paradigms," according to Michel Gauquelin in his book, *Neo-Astrology*. "The paradigms are 'universally' accepted scientific truths which, for a time, provide the community of researchers with a model for all the problems and all their solutions." That is, until they break down, which is what's happening all around us today.

With the advent of modern science about a hundred years ago, other intellectual disciplines disowned and abandoned astrology as mere entertainment, especially when respectable astrologers began oversimplifying astrology with their emphasis on the Sun signs.

For example, during the 20th century it has been rare indeed for a respectable astronomer - let alone an economist, businessman or politician, attorney, physician or psychologist - to publicly admit using astrology. Starting in the late 1900's astrology had been relegated to one-line conversational openers ("Hey, what's your sign"), three-line summaries next to the comic strips in daily newspapers, and an carnival image of clandestine meetings with soothsayers wearing turbans, burning incense and waving crystals.

The worlds of modern science and medicine, business and finance were changing so rapidly that astrologers just couldn't keep up ... until recently.

My first exposure to Kuhn's work was in Marilyn Ferguson's 1982 classic, *The Aquarian Conspiracy*, shortly after leaving the Financial News Network.

Ferguson says, "A paradigm is a framework of thought (from the Greek word *paradigma*, 'pattern'). A paradigm is a scheme for understanding and explaining certain aspects of reality. Although Kuhn was writing about science, the term has been widely adopted. People speak of educational paradigms, paradigms for city planning, the paradigm shift in medicine, and so on."

Astrology is no exception, because astrology is definitely experiencing an acute case of its paradigm shifting, you might even call it a *cosmic psychotic split!* Today we are in the middle of an emerging new vision where anything is possible and the astrological sciences can give you a competitive edge.

SUDDENLY: THE PARADIGM SHIFTS & A NEW ASTROLOGY EMERGES!

At the beginning of the 20th century Einstein's Theory of Relativity challenged the rigidities of a Newtonian worldview, opening the door to *seeing* many other inconsistencies between the old and a newer, more flexible reality. With these struggles comes crisis and a breakdown, as the old is pitted against the new in a battle for the minds of the public.

SUCCESS TIP: PREDICTING YOUR FUTURE IN A WORLD OF CHAOS.
In the next several years many new money-making opportunities will be open to you if you are able to "keep your head when all men about you are losing theirs and blaming it on you." We're in an age of *Future Shock* and success will come to those able to see beyond the intense personal and international crises.

Very few will be able to see in advance the structure of the emerging new social order - and the role of astrology in it - because large numbers of people will be overwhelmed by personal crises, as these powerful forces break down the old order of the social structures around them. They won't see the light at the end of the tunnel because it is still under construction.

Psychologically, it is difficult enough to grasp the meaning of a *personal* crisis *when you're in the middle it*, let alone try to understand a global paradigm shift when you're in a personal crisis! Most people only grasp the meaning of life's events in the rear-view mirror, long after the fact. Many never do.

If *you* are going to profit from opportunities during this emerging new world order, *you must keep an open mind to everything, including the predictive abilities of astrology during the chaos.* Otherwise, like many others, you may not see the rapid changes coming in the next several years ... until it's too late.

For the key change-agents - not just the Einsteins and other leaders in the sciences, but hopefully *you* - "enlightenment" comes suddenly, Zen-like, with a total, immediate comprehension of the new reality. As the scientist Kuhn said, the new paradigm will "occur all at once ... not figured out," but seen in a flash.

For many others, change comes very slowly, in what the psychologist William James calls the "educational variety." Here change is slow, evolutionary. It is also painful and obstructionist. Vested interests struggle to defend and modify the existing order. Or attempt to patch together the old and the new paradigms, often an impossible task. Meanwhile, all this is happening amid massive *MegaTrend* changes, as Naisbett defined them, changes that are coming at us at mind-blowing speeds, in what Alvin Toffler calls *Future Shock!*

THE 5 KEY FORCES TRANSFORMING MODERN ASTROLOGY

From my perspective, the bottom-line is that today there are five major forces simultaneously driving this paradigm shift, creating a new astrological paradigm

THE PARADIGM SHIFT

for the 21st century. These five forces will be discussed in detail in the next several chapters. They are:

> **OVERVIEW: THE 5 FORCES CREATING A NEW ASTROLOGY**
>
> **ONE: THE POWER OF WALL STREET MONEY,** beginning with the clear impact of J.P. Morgan, W.D. Gann and several leaders using astrology, along with other natural cycles, in their personal and business decisions and in trading in the stock market. This grounding element is the earth's power.
>
> **TWO: MODERN PSYCHOLOGY AND MEDICINE,** especially the incredible works of Dr. Carl G. Jung creating a science of psychology and integrating it with mythology and astrology. The psyche is the element of water power.
>
> **THREE: SCIENCE AND COMPUTER TECHNOLOGY,** particularly, the scientific correlation studies of Dr. Michel Gauquelin, a French statistician and psychologist, who researched 500,000 birth charts of successful men and women for over 40 years. This rational element is air power.
>
> **FOUR: HI-TECH MYTHOLOGY AND SPIRITUALITY,** notably Joseph Campbell whose works were built on Jung's mythological studies, reflecting the human psyche in the larger spiritual archetypes of the Collective Unconscious. Fire power is the element of living with passion.
>
> **FIVE: THE POWER OF CREATIVE ACTION,** with special reference to the teaching and writings of Dr. Roger von Oech, a management consultant who teaches *creative thinking* to Corporate America. This element of creative energy transcends the others, acting as the unifying force.

    The first four of these forces - earth, water, air and fire - relate directly to the four basic *elements* of life that you have, no doubt, historically encountered in the sciences and traditional religions as well as in astrology. The fifth element is that elusive power binding the other four elements together. It is what the eastern mystics have long called the Tao, the great mysterious life force possessed by each of us.
    The simultaneous impact of these five powerful forces is creating a powerful synergistic effect forcing a revolution in modern astrology. Out of this paradigm shift will emerge a new astrology for the 21st Century. Let's examine some of the key elements of the transformation that is in progress now, for clues to the new astrology of the future.

BEFORE YOU READ THE NEXT FIVE CHAPTERS ...

The next five chapters of Part One of this book review the general context of change that has been remolding modern astrology since the turn of the century.

While I personally believe it's important for you to understand these five forces transforming the field of astrology *before moving on,* you may, nevertheless, want to *quickly* peruse these chapters and then move on to Part Two, "How It Works," and the more specific processes of how astrology can be applied to make money in your business, management, financial and investment decisions.

TREND #1
THE POWER OF WALL STREET MONEY

The 1st Force Reshaping Modern Astrology Is
THE KILLER INSTINCT & THE BOTTOM LINE OF WALL STREET & CORPORATE AMERICA.
The "Secret Conspiracy" in Business & Financial Astrology

> **THE BOTTOM-LINE:** Although kept relatively quiet and secretive, astrological forecasting has become an essential part of the decision-making processes for a significant number of logical, tough-minded, left-brained leaders in the business and financial world, beginning a century ago with J. Pierpont Morgan and W.D. Gann, the founder of Wall Street's technical market charting, and continuing today throughout America.

"J.P. Morgan, the world's biggest financier, drove the world before him because he had astrology behind him," said Evangeline Adams in 1926, summarizing her experiences as Morgan's astrologer in her autobiography, written several years after his death.

Adams should know. Morgan frequently visited her for astrological advice. Not just because Adams came from a *good* Bostonian family, a direct descendant of U.S. President John Quincy Adams. Nor because she was a attractive young lady in her early thirties. But because her predictions proved quite accurate and were worth the price, as much as $5,000 for a consultation.

ST. PADDY'S DAY FIRE GIVES MORGAN'S ASTROLOGER A HOT START

Adams gained considerable public notoriety right from the time she arrived in New York City on March 16th of 1899. That day she took up residence in the famed Windsor Hotel. As good fortune would have it, on her first day in town, Adams had an opportunity to do an astrology consultation for the hotel manager, warning that he was, "under the worst possible combination of planets - conditions terrifying in their unfriendliness."

> **SUCCESS FACT:** During the St. Patrick's Day parade the next day, the Windsor Hotel burnt to the ground, killing several people. The New York City newspapers carried the hotel manager's comments about Adams' fateful predictions ... and Adam's astrological career got off to a hot start!

Around that time, the Morgan family were financing the likes of such activities as the U.S. Steel Corporation, the Great Northern & Pacific Railroad and the Boer War. Morgan was frequently seen in the company of Henry James, Rudyard Kipling and Mark Twain, as well as Andrew Carnegie and other leaders of Wall Street and Corporate America.

Morgan also saw Adams. Like many other leaders grounded in the real world of business, he initially viewed astrology with considerable skepticism.

"The first time he came to my studio," writes Adams, "his attitude was frankly one of curiosity tinged with suspicion. I had a heavy Chinese screen in one corner of my studio; and I remember how Mr. Morgan pulled his huge frame out of the chair and looked behind the screen before beginning the interview."

After the first session Morgan regularly sought Adams astrological advice, which he affirmed in his famous remark, "Millionaires don't hire astrologers, billionaires do." He continued on a regular basis until his death in 1913.

Adams also advised James Hill, the father of the America railroad industry and three successive Presidents of the New York Stock Exchange. "Dozens of men in the 'street' whose names are known wherever stocks are sold avail themselves of my monthly indications. And fully one third of the people who come to see me and write me from distant points ask me how they can make their fortunes in the stock market."

WALL STREET CYCLES & TECHNICAL ANALYSIS

Astrology began 6,000 years as a practical tool for farmers trying to get an edge against the unpredictabilities of nature. Think of the first astrologers as the forerunners of today's television weathermen. That's why the old Farmer's Almanac has been one of the most popular books of all time. Then around 1895, William Delbert Gann, a mathematical genius and astrologer, added a new twist to the old game.

Gann may be lesser known to the general public, but Gann had an even greater impact than J.P. Morgan on the use of astrology in the financial world. Gann developed a system of tracking astrological and other natural cycles as a way of predicting turning points and directions in the commodities and stock markets. Between 1895 and his death in 1955, he became one of the most successful traders on Wall Street and Chicago Board of Trade, personally accumulating more than $50,000,000 by the end of WWII.

> **SUCCESS FACTS: W.D. Gann viewed life itself as one universal whole. There were no conflicts between his astrology, religious fundamentalism, natural law, mathematics ... and getting rich. His techniques were based on *timing cycles* which he observed scientifically as *laws of nature*, and then he converted into mathematical formulas.**
>
> **Gann's world-view was based on strong religious convictions, he was raised in the strong traditions of a strict Texas Methodist family. He liberally quoted the Bible throughout his works. If you're even a bit religious, you might be inclined to quote the bible, "God certainly works in mysterious ways, his wonders to perform" ... and see Gann as an excellent example of God's prosperity at work.**

Gann made his first speculative commodities trade in 1902. By 1910, at the age of 32, Gann was offering an investment advisory service for the steep price of $3,000 to $4,000 annually per subscriber, without a computer or Xerox machine.

Today, Gann's scientific techniques are the basis of all *technical market analysis* systems used nationally by investors and brokers trading in the stock and commodities markets.

Morgan and Gann gave astrology a new, high level of respectability within the American business and financial world, a credibility that remains strong to this day. I know one successful entrepreneur/astrologer who claims that Donald Regan, former U.S. Secretary of the Treasury and President of the New York Stock Exchange once said that 47% of Wall Street brokers use astrology. Investors and brokers may not admit it publicly, any more than they will openly discuss visits to their ministers and attorneys, but many rely on astrologers as often as economists. *Whatever works!*

In fact, one solid prediction by a respected astrologer like Adams or Gann is often considered more valuable than those of many of our leading economists. Most clients, however, don't acknowledge it publicly, especially since the public outcry toward President Reagan's use of astrologers, which raised old fears that the our country was being controlled by some outside, possibly even evil forces. It's okay to talk to an economist, attorney or political strategist who might well influence or even direct the President in policy matters, but God forbid that he should talk to an astrologer!

TRACKING THE UPS & DOWNS OF THE S&P 500 WITH MARS & VENUS

Gann's systematic study of astrology and the mathematical *laws of nature* governing the financial markets has led to considerable research. For example, in the famous 1960 book, *Success Through A Positive Mental Attitude*, Napoleon Hill and Clement Stone begin one section endorsing the analysis of cycles:

> **MONEY TIP: You can "make a fortune and achieve your aims by understanding cycles and trends. Many years ago Paul Raymond, Vice President in charge of loans for the American National Bank and Trust Company of Chicago, rendered a service to his customers. He sent them a copy of Dewey and Dankin's book, *Cycles*. Subsequently many of these clients made fortunes. They learned and understood the theory of business cycles and trends."**

Napoleon Hill's first book, *Think And Grow Rich*, is a classic based on Andrew Carnegie's "Science of Success." Clement Stone made his fortune in the insurance business, published *Success* magazine. He also funded some of the work of Edward Dewey's *Foundation For The Study Of Cycles*, which has been dedicated to this emerging new science of cycles since the Thirties when Dewey, a former Department of Commerce economist created the Foundation. Originally, Dewey was part of a Depression era government team charged with developing techniques of predicting economic boom-bust cycles.

"For over a million years man has been trying to predict his future," begins Edward Dewey 1971 book, *Cycles, The Mysterious Forces That Trigger Events*. "He has always failed - and his failures are buried in the dust of history."

> **PREDICTING ECONOMIC & BUSINESS CYCLES: You should be aware of this new Science of Cycles that began with Edward Dewey. As he said, today, "working quietly behind the scenes, thousands of scientist in fields as unrelated as history, botany, anthropology, mammalogy, terrestrial magnetism, sociology, and economics - to name a few - are accumulating facts and figures that promise to make this age-old dream of foretelling the future at least a partial reality. A new science which deals with the behavior of events recurring at reasonably regular intervals throughout the universe may enable us to predict, scientifically and accurately, the events of tomorrow."**

For example, my background as a real estate executive made me especially interested in the Foundation's explanation of the 18.2 year cycle in real estate activity, tracked for 300 years since 1795 and first identified by Samuel Benner in 1875. The Foundation's work has resulted in their tracking thousands of cycles, and interestingly, many diverse ones have common patterns that generally improve the predictability of events and turning points.

Although the Foundation, as well as its editors, contributors and supporters tend to ignore and disassociate themselves from astrology (astronomy is acceptable), their focus on cycles and trends makes the Foundation's research *essential* reading for the new breed of 21st Century astrologers.

Matrix Software also provides *Time Cycles,* a computer version of 4,300 tested geophysical, market and economic indicators, including historic Dow-Jones Averages, various industrial production and sales, tides and other lunar activity, plus a host of natural and planetary cycles. Richard Mogey, Director of the Cycles Foundation says, "I can't recommend this program highly enough."

FINANCIAL ASTROLOGERS FOR THE 21st CENTURY

Today there are many astrologers specializing in the fields of business and financial astrology and astro-economics, most notable, Lt.Cmdr. **David Williams,** an engineer with Con Edison and author of *Astro-Economics* and *Financial Astrology.* The American Federation of Astrologers called Williams the *Dean of American Astro-Economics,* noting that for 20 years he "scored an 80% accuracy rating" in predicting the economy and the market. In addition to his scientific and technical writings he has written extensively on this subject in popular journals. Williams' 1982 book *Financial Astrology* reviewed, among other things:
- **major economic and business cycles,**
- **the effects of solar and interplanetary energy on the communications, power and healthcare industries,**
- **fundamental analysis of individual corporations,**
- **and general forecasting of the stock markets.**

William's book has an incredible wealth of historical references on key figures in the financial astrology field as well as discussions of their methods and the results. He includes the classic works of **Louise McWhirter**, *Astrology and Stock Market Forecasting,* **L.J. Jensen,** *Astro-cycles and Speculative Markets,* and many, many other key leaders in the financial astrology, cycles research, technical analysis and charting. This book is essential reading for anyone in today's fast-paced world of business and finance.

Joan McEvers recently edited another major book, *Financial Astrology For The 1990s,* with articles by nine excellent authors, each of whom is a practicing professional in the field of business, economics and financial astrology. This compendium is a *must see* overview of the current state of the new Money Astrology. Some of the topics included in the book are:
- **A Primer on Market Forecasting,** Michael Munkasey
- **Predicting The Dow,** Carol Mull
- **Commodities Trading and Technical Analysis,** Jeanne Long
- **The Gann Technique,** Judy Johns
- **Charting Organizations; U.S.A. & N.Y.S.E.,** Pat Esclavon Hardy
- **The Real Estate Process,** Georgia Stathis
- **Astrological Analysis of Public Corporations,** Georgia Stathis
- **Predicting The Economy,** Robert Cole

Other financial experts and teachers active in the field include **Jeanne Long**, commodities trader, publisher of the annual *Traders' Astrology Almanac* and *AstroTech.* In *Financial Astrology For The 1990's*, Long cautions, "Do not take planetary signals without confirmation from technical signals."

Another highly respected leader in the field, **Larry Pesavento,** is a former Chicago Commodities Board trader now operating from offices in Pismo Beach, California. Pesavento publishes a monthly newsletter, *AstroCycles*, on trends in the commodities and stock markets, and has written three key books on financial astrology, including *Planetary Harmonics of Speculative Markets.*

THE POWER OF WALL STREET MONEY

One of the better known experts on financial astrology is **Arch Crawford**, known as "The Wall Street Astrologer." A former Merrill Lynch market analyst, Crawford is highly respected on Wall Street and has published a successful market newsletter, *Crawford Perspectives*, since 1977.

> **SUCCESS FACTS:** Recently the *Timer Digest* awarded Crawford with the distinction of "1992 Long-Term Timer of the Year." *Timer Digest* earlier noted that Crawford forecasts trends using 28 different technical market indicators ... quoting him, "the astronomic work, as powerful as it is, is still in a very early developmental stage, and it pays to keep two fingers on the pulse of the market through technical analysis." This astro-analyst predicted the 1987 market crash.

Interestingly, right after the 1987 stock market crash, astrologers whose main focus is on money, economics and finance also started an annual forum, *The World Conference on Astro-Economics*, which is further evidence of the paradigm shift currently reshaping the field of astrology. Other major national conferences on the emerging new astrology have been sponsored by the *New York Center for Astrology* and the *Global Research Forum*.

Henry Weingarten, a financial astrologer with 25 years experience, is the managing director of *The Astrologers Fund, Inc.*, a multi-million dollar private investment vehicle for high net-worth investors, and founder of the New York Center for Astrology. He is the first astrologer *officially* hired by a registered Wall Street brokerage firm, with the title of Executive Astrological Analyst.

Bill Meridian is another major investment fund manager who also publishes a newsletter, *Cycles Research*. A former Vice President of Paine-Webber, he was originally trained as a psychotherapist. Currently based in Abu Dhabi, Meridian developed a computer program for market trading, *AstroAnalyst*, with Robert Hand, and the new *Stock Market Program* with Alphee Lavoie of AIR Software.

INVESTMENT ADVISORS, BUSINESS CONSULTANTS, TRADERS & MORE!

Several other financial astrologers are also publishing market newsletters and books. Many of their works are reviewed in detail in Williams' *Financial Astrology* and Pesavento's *Astro-cycles, The Trader's Viewpoint*.

Mason Sexton started his timing newsletter, *Harmonic Research* in 1984 after solid work with Morgan Stanley & Co., Salomon Brothers and Mitchell Hutchins.

Larry Berg's *Whole Earth Forecaster* has been published since 1981, providing timing advice on short and long-term stock and commodity trading.

Carol Mull is an active market trader. Her excellent publications include, *750 OTC Stocks, S&P's 500* and a newsletter, *The Market Forecast Letter*. A financial accountant, Mull organized the Conference on Astro-Timing Techniques for Traders, and co-founded the World Conference on Astro-Economics.

Tim Bost, a management consultant and astrologer, publishes *Financial Cycles* in South Carolina. He is a former marketing and advertising executive.

Raymond Merriman, a securities broker, publishes a newsletter, *MMA Cycles Report*, and he has authored several books on stock market astrology, including *The Gold Book: GeoCosmic Correlations To Gold Prices*.

Norman Winski, publisher of *Astro-Trend*, is a Chicago commodities trader who relies heavily on financial astrology. Winski now owns the financial astrology library of J. P. Morgan's astrologer.

In addition, there are many other business and economic astrologers:

Richard Houck, a Washington, D.C. management consultant and astrologer, is the managing partner of ARC Associates. Nationally known for his political forecasting, Houck's experience includes Arthur Andersen & Co. management, and senior information officer of computer security at Intelsat satellite network.

Pat Esclavon Hardy, President of Energies, Trends, Cycles, Inc., is a market research analyst and business consultant previously on staff with the U.S. National Geologic Survey. Her national and international "Economic Forecast" in Llewellyn's annual *Moon Sign Book* is perceptive, informative and well-written.

Grace Morris, co-founder of the World Conference on Astro-Economics and the author of *Working With Businesses*, is a Chicago psychotherapist, astrologer, and the owner of a business advisory service.

Georgia Stathis is a Bay Area astrologer, realtor and management consultant specializing in corporate and real estate transactions.

There are many other financial astrologers throughout the United States and internationally, such as **Charles Harvey** and **Graham Bates** in England.

These are just a few examples of the new generation of Money A$trologers. Astrology is an integral part of their trading in the securities markets, in their work as corporate consultants and as personal advisors to investors, business executives and entrepreneurs.

WARNING: THE NEW A$TROLOGERS *ARE* FROM DIFFERENT PLANET$!

As we'll see in the coming chapters, today's astrologers often appear to be coming from planets at opposite ends of the galaxy - as different as the officers and crew of the *Star Trek* spaceship, the Enterprise.

Is your astrologer a Vulcan, Betazoid or Klingon? You certainly can't tell by *looking* at them. You must look within, listen to their words, observe their actions. This is critical information for you. Here is one of the main differences between these polar opposites on the astrological spectrum:

. **Financial Astrologers** focus on *mass psychology*, relying on the collective reactions of groups which can be predicted *en mass.* As Gann would say, "There's nothing mysterious about my predictions. I use algebra and geometry and tell exactly by their theory of cycles when a certain thing is going to occur again." The focus is the continuity and predictability of groups and the masses. Individual psychology interests them only as it may help in determining their personal trading styles and their choice of markets to specialize in.

. **Personal Astrologers** focus on the *individual psychology*. The contrast between them and the financial astrologers is most evident in Carl Jung's comment, "The great events of world history are, at bottom, profoundly unimportant. The essential thing is the life of the individual. This alone makes history, here alone do the great transformations take place." In another context, Anthony Robbins succinctly expressed this emphasis on freedom, "The past does not predict the future." With these personal astrologers, the focus is on change within a *specific individual,* rather than predicting *mass* trends, and on the future and personal freedoms, rather than predictions based on *past* trends ... *individual freedoms in the future versus mass trends from the past.*

A$TROLOGY 2001: BOLDLY GOING WHERE NO ONE HAS GONE BEFORE!

The bottom-line is that while both perspectives are essential to a balanced way of life, you must be aware of these and other major differences among today's astrologers. We will examine all of the variations in depth in the following chapters - their style, education and choice of data bases. You will need this information when hiring your astrological consultants, and in order to understand and profit from the emerging new Money A$trology.

TREND #2
THE POWER OF MODERN PSYCHOLOGY

The 2nd Force Reshaping Modern Astrology Is
JUNGIAN PSYCHOLOGY & PSYCHOTHERAPY
YOUR DNA/GENES *ARE* IN SYNC WITH THE STARS!
Modern Psychology Is Based On 6,000 Years of Astrology

THE BOTTOM-LINE: With the 20th Century development of psychology as a science, astrology has regained considerable credibility as a tool in analyzing human behavior. The powerful influence of Dr. Carl G. Jung - himself a master astrologer - has encouraged many psychologists and other healthcare professionals to explore new astrological techniques. In addition, many astrologers are now studying modern psychology.

Astrological techniques had been used in the practice of medicine for a long time. For example, astrology continues as an integral part of the Vedic medical tradition practiced in India for thousands of years, as noted in the work of Deepak Chopra, M.D., author of *Quantum Healing* and *Perfect Health*. In addition, one astrologer I know has, over the years, helped physicians select dates and times for 4,000 surgical procedures using cycles of the Moon and other astrological influences. Research studies support the fact that excessive bleeding is more likely to occur during some Moon phases rather than others.

Unfortunately, astrology was very slow in responding to the rapid technological advances that began revolutionizing modern medicine in the 20th Century. The *scientific and technological* basis of astrology remained relatively stagnant until the 1970's and the advent of personal computers. Before that, there was a potential danger that astrology would become as anachronistic as blood-letting and leeches, as astrology fell from grace among the professions and into the Sun-sign columns on the comic pages of the tabloids.

THE DEATH & REBIRTH OF ASTROLOGY: As a skeptic (or a closet believer who is legitimately worried about public criticism) you would have been in good company during most of the 20th Century. Not too long ago "astrology was scarcely worth attacking," according to Anthony West in *The Case For Astrology*. "Astrology is already dead. It has been dead so long it no longer stinks,' declared one Dr. Charles Arthur Mercier in 1913."

Moreover, West notes that "in 1976, 186 scientists, 19 of them Nobel Prize-winners, endorsed a manifesto called 'Objections to Astrology'. The signers recommended a united front and a concerted effort to stamp out the insidious, ancient superstition once and for all; 'otherwise reputable' publishers were exhorted to stop publishing books by 'astrological charlatans'." Despite all this opposition, the new astrology is rapidly developing scientific credibility.

Fortunately, the development of modern psychology as a science throughout the 20th century, has *forced* astrology to search for a new identity. For this impetus, the astrologers owe a special thanks the *cutting edge* works of Dr. Carl Jung and his analytical psychology.

CARL JUNG, THE FATHER OF MODERN ASTROLOGY

When the complete history of modern astrology is written, Dr. Carl G. Jung, the Swiss psychologist and physician, will be clearly identified as the dominant individual triggering the transformation of astrology during this 20th century paradigm shift. In addition to his work in medicine and psychology, Carl Jung influenced changes in two key areas related to astrology:

First: the left-brain or rational side, with the work of Dr. Michel Gauquelin, scientist, statistician and psychologist, which will be discussed later, and

Second: the right-brain or intuitive side, with the mythic and creative work of Joseph Campbell, which will be reviewed in the chapter on the third major force causing the paradigm shift in modern astrology.

Today, the legacy of Carl Jung clearly remains one of the dominant force in astrology, as it has been for almost a century.

JUNG: ASTROLOGERS WERE THE "ORIGINAL PSYCHOLOGISTS."
Carl Jung had very strong convictions about and respect for the power of astrology and astrologers throughout its 6,000 year history.

In a 1930 address delivered in Munich, Jung acknowledged that the roots of psychology were in astrology, "Astrology is assured recognition from psychology, without further restrictions, because *astrology represents the summation of all the psychological knowledge of antiquity.*"

"The fact that it is possible to construct, in adequate fashion, a person's character from the date of his nativity, shows the relative validity of astrology," Jung continued. "Whatever is born or done this moment, has the qualities of this moment in time."

Jung called the unseen bond or connection between the individual and the universe, synchronicity, "the simultaneous occurrence of two meaningful but not casually connected events," things that cannot be dismissed as merely coincidental, even if they are polar opposites.

Jung's concept of *synchronicity* is a reflection of Einstein's unified theory of relativity, with the simultaneous and unexplained turning of "unrelated" electrons. The idea of synchronicity, however, has its roots in many ancient traditions.

The ancient phrase, "the psyche *is* the cosmos," refers to the *synchronistic* bond between you and the universe, between your inner power - your *inner astrologer* - and the electromagnetic energies of the planets. Synchronicity has also been paraphrased in the writings of many great thinkers, including Meister Eckhert, the medieval Christian mystic, Deepak Chopra, the physician trained in both Eastern and Western medicine, Black Elk, a native Indian spiritual leader and the great Zenmasters ... as well as Jung's analytical psychology.

DR. JUNG, PSYCHOLOGIST and MASTER ASTROLOGER

Astrology was more than a subject of academic and scientific interest to Jung. Although it was not common knowledge, Jung was a master astrologer, frequently using astrology as a diagnostic tool with his patients. In fact, in one research study Jung claimed a 97% accuracy for his astrological findings.

However, in the early days of Jung's work, the association with astrology was not considered good for the image of the emerging new field of psychology, which was struggling to develop its own scientific credibility.

As a result, Jung's use of astrology was kept relatively quiet. Jung's colleagues believed that any link between the emerging new science of psychology and astrology would taint the image of professionalism and scientific

THE POWER OF MODERN PSYCHOLOGY

credibility sought by psychologists. Therefore, a safe distance was maintained between the two in public, while psychology developed itself as a scientific discipline. Later, the same demand for a scientific professionalism was to spill over into the new community of astrologers.

> **JUNG'S ASTROLOGICAL RESEARCH SCORES 97% ACCURACY**
> Dr. Carl Jung was a master astrologer. In the "Historic Astrology" column of a recent Llewellyn's Calendar, Deter Damian writes, "The eminent Swiss psychologist Carl Gustav Jung demonstrated astrology's remarkable predictive capacity by a statistical experiment using standard astrological procedure and involving 1,932 horoscopes. His results scored 97% accuracy. Jung who referred to astrology as 'the summation of all psychological knowledge of antiquity,' applied it to formulate his theories about human behavior, casting horoscopes to aid his psychoanalysis of patients. An increasing number of psychologists are following Jung's lead."

Astrology has certainly needed an major *image make-over* for some time. Beginning in the late 19th century, many astrologers began writing for newspapers as a way of increasing their exposure and bank accounts, writing relatively useless astrological columns superficially based on the Sun-signs. This has left many observers with the obvious impression that astrology is little more than fluffy, light-hearted entertainment on the comics pages of the daily news, but hardly a serious guide for personal and business decision-making.

REVOLUTION: THE LEADING EDGE OF THE PARADIGM SHIFT

By the early 1970s this image began to change. Three major trends began surfacing that have accelerated the paradigm shift, occurring about the same time Thomas Kuhn published his classic, *The Structure Of Scientific Revolutions:*

One: Dr. Michel Gauquelin's psychological research studies have been one major factor, giving astrology a scientific basis. His scientific research will be discussed in the next chapter.

Two: Joseph Campbell's scholarly works on mythology have given additional respectability to the subtle connections Carl Jung saw between mythology, psychology and astrology. They are the basis of the hugely popular mythological films of Lucas and Spielberg. Campbell's influence will be discussed below in the chapter on the fourth force creating the new astrology.

Three: And equally important, the development of relatively inexpensive personal computer hardware and software systems has freed a new generation of astrologers from the drudgery of numbers-crunching, allowing - indeed, *forcing* - them to dig deeper into the underlying *psychological meaning* of astrological cycles and events.

THE NEW BREED: "HYPHENATES" ... ASTROLOGERS *PLUS SOMETHING!*

With these dramatic changes, a new generation of astrologers has begun to emerge, what I now call the *hyphenate*, a term borrowed from the entertainment industry with its *writer-directors* and *actor-producers*. We also see hyphenates in the medical field, which has invented fancy new terms like *psychoneuro-immuniology*, apparently because a simpler hyphenate suggesting the *mind-body* connection would sound a bit too *new age.*

These combinations reflect a growing cross-over of disciplines. Today's astrologers - *the hyphenates* - are typically an astrologer *plus something else:*

. **Astro-Psychologists:** existing astrologers are now being given the opportunity to return to their historic roots as *quasi-psychologists,* following the innovative path taken by Carl Jung.

. **Psychological Astronomers:** large numbers of professionals trained in psychology have begun taking a much greater interest in the clinical and therapeutic value of astrology. In his book *The Night Speaks,* the astrologer Steven Forrest refers to himself as a *psychological astronomer!*

A SHARP CONTRAST: PSYCHOLOGISTS vs. MARKET TRADERS

Astro-Counselors: in many ways these *astro-therapists* (astrologers into *individual* psychology and mythology) are substantially different than the *astro-traders* (those *into mass* psychology, the stock market, astro-economics and financial astrology). The differences are substantial. They have such different goals and clients, they work with different issues, techniques and data bases, that it is hard to see the common professional thread (other than *astronomical events and energies),* as we do in the professions of medicine, teaching and the law. The commodities trader-astrologer Larry Pesavento remarked in *Wall Street Computer Review,* "If you told me you were a Gemini, I would have no idea of what that's supposed to mean. Our interest in planetary movements is based entirely on ... the direction of the markets."

Financial Astronomers: one publisher has boldly suggested to me that the experts in business, finance and the stock markets should completely eliminate the term astrology from their work. Instead of calling themselves financial *astrologers,* use the term financial *astronomers* to focus attention on their use of an astronomic data base in the world of finance, and thus downplay the *astrology* connection, in the same way Jung down-played his work in astrology. Weingarten comes close with his definition of "astrology as a mathematical psychology based on astronomy."

We should again mention the many other *hyphenate-astrologers* who are *already* out there practicing and earning a living today:
. Career Consultant-Astrologers,
. Realtor-Astrologers
. Personnel Director-Astrologers,
. Advertising Agent-Astrologers,
. Stock Broker-Astrologers,
. Management Consultant-Astrologers, and others.

In yet another context, Dr. Gauquelin simply used the terms *neo-astrologers* and *astral astrologers* to describe the new astrologer. In my view, these are all excellent examples of this exciting new breed of 21st Century astrologers.

THE NEW BREED of "PSYCHOLOGICAL ASTRONOMERS!"

Here are a few more examples of the key leaders who have already emerged during the paradigm shift, men and women whose work clearly reflects the historic, synchronistic bond between psychology and astrology:

. **Robert Hand** is the founder of Astrolabe, the primary astrological research and computer services center on the East Coast. Hand is also the author of *Planets in Transit,* a brilliant handbook on the cycles of psychological behavior.

. **Dane Rudhyar**, a prolific writer and contemporary of the psychologist, Carl Rogers, introduced many astrologers to "person-centered" astrology, as an extension of Rogers' person-centered psychology.

. **Noel Tyl**, a Harvard graduate in psychology is one of the leading teachers of the science of astrology. Tyl's works include the 12-volume *Principles and Practice of Astrology;* he predicted the Gulf War and other major events.

. **Liz Green**, a British psychologist and astrologer draws heavily on the structure and processes of Jungian psychology.

THE POWER OF MODERN PSYCHOLOGY

. **Stephen Arroyo** is a trained therapist and represents the new generation of astrologers integrating astrology with Jungian psychology. Arroyo wrote *Astrology, Karma and Transformation*, and several other brilliant texts.

. **Jamie Binder**, a Chicago personnel consultant who wrote *Planets In Work*, as a comprehensive guide to career, business and employment decisions.

. **Maritha Pottenger**, another professional psychotherapist and the author of *Complete Horoscope Interpretation*, is also on the professional staff at ACS, the Astro Communication Services in San Diego, which was Dr. Gauquelin's home here in this country.

. **Steven Forrest,** an astrologer and author or co-authored several books, *The Changing Sky, The Inner Sky, Stagnates* and *The Night Speaks*.

. **Marlene Rathgeb**, a marketing executive with a major New York magazine publisher, wrote an excellent book, *Success Signs*, as a guide for understanding personality types in selecting various careers.

. **John Townley**, a career counselor and recording engineer, wrote *Astrological Life Cycles, A Planetary Guide to Personal and Career Opportunities.*

These are just a few key individuals, along with the financial astrologers, on the leading edge of a whole new generation of *hyphenate-astrologers*.

THE BOTTOM-LINE: A NEW SECRET "CONSPIRACY"

These leaders represent a new generation of astrological teachers and writers, men and women who are also trained in the fields of psychotherapy, Jungian psychology and the real world of business.

While there is a *world* of separation between these psychologically-oriented astrologers and the astro-economists, astro-traders and financial astrologers, they do have a common bond in the astronomy of the stars, a bond that reflects the message in Ferguson's book, *The Aquarian Conspiracy*. We are all part of a network that "has already enlisted the minds, hearts and resources of some of our most advanced thinkers from every corner of American society." The new astrology of the 21st Century is becoming a large bed filled with strange bed-fellows indeed.

As this trend accelerates, you can expect to see even more *hyphenates* - astrologers taking university degrees in psychology, as well as more therapists, counselors and psychologists using astrology as a diagnostic and predictive tool to provide valuable *second opinions*. And we have certainly seen large numbers of *securities traders practicing astrology, using mass psychology*.

The collective, synergistic force of these professionals represents a powerful new wave of raw energy pushing the field of astrology directly into the leading edge of the paradigm shift and on into the 21st century.

THE MARINE CORPS BUILDS MEN
"The successful battle is waged first in the mind," commands one of The Marine Corps' powerful ads in the *Leatherneck* magazine. Both the art of warfare and the art of living are at bottom psychological ... It all begins in *your* brain.

The Marine Corps gave me my first lesson in the critical importance of psychology on the battlefield of life. I was put to the test, as one of "the few, the proud," a U.S. Marine staff sergeant. Today I know we all share a common battlefield ... the larger paradigm shift that is also a battle waged first in our collective minds. Its message comes through your *inner astrologer*.

Listen, get into action, lead.

WHAT'S THE DIFFERENCE BETWEEN ASTROLOGY & ASTRONOMY?

"Astrology," wrote Ralph Waldo Emerson, "is astronomy brought to earth and applied to the affairs of men and women," an interpretation of the impact that cosmic cycles and events have on individuals and groups.

Astronomy is the science of celestial *observations*, such as the *facts* necessary for NASA and JPL to navigate the Voyager 2 satellite on a twisting course through space for 12 years (August 20, 1977 to August, 1989), guiding this 0.9 ton space probe so accurately that it passed within 4,950 *kilometers* of the planet Neptune ... which is approximately 2.6 *billion* miles from the Earth!

Now that's a bull's-eye!

The work of the *personal* astrologers takes the astronomers' observations *one key step further*, based on their conviction that "the psyche *is* the cosmos." Astrologers believe there is a synchronistic connection between the cycles of these remote celestial phenomenon and the behavior of individual humans.

That's one quantum leap modern astronomers refuse to make.

The new astrologers, however, no longer believe that interplanetary electro-magnetic energies and events *control* humans, only that there is a mysterious *synchronicity* between the two.

Free will still exists. *You still make decisions.*

You should also be aware that Carl Sagan, America's best known astronomer, has some major reservations about astrology.

"Astronomy is a science - the study of the Universe as it is. Astrology is a pseudo-science - a claim, in the absence of good evidence, that the other planets affect our daily lives," Sagan says in his 1980 book, *Cosmos*. Sagan was justifiably critical of the popular astrology found in the tabloids and the comic pages of most newspapers.

In recent years Sagan has been assisting NASA with a $10 million annual research program searching the universe for radio messages from alien civilizations on distant planets that may be attempting to contact the Earth.

Today's *astrologers* are also becoming much more scientific. Like JPL and NASA astronomers, they insist on working with *the facts.*

One segment of Williams' extensive research indicates that during the 221 years between 1761 and 1982, transits of Jupiter and Saturn - with its 19.859 year cycle - have demonstrated a 83% accuracy in predicting turning points in *long-term* business cycles.

Pesavento's computer research is another excellent example. Among his other projects, he tested 636 aspects of Venus and Uranus for a 90 year period between 1898 and 1987 and concluded that these aspects had a 92% accuracy in determining *short-term* turning points in the stock markets.

That's like putting the Voyager within 4,950 kilometers of Neptune. Better yet, that's like putting $4,950 in the bank ... *yours!*

In many ways, these new astrologers have a lot in common with Carl Sagan, and Carl Jung before him. They are now demanding that all astrologers become more scientific and more professionally responsible. And their own work is setting a powerful example for the new generation.

Today, I am convinced that Sagan would arrive at a different conclusion if he seriously reviewed the recent works of Michel Gauquelin and Percy Seymour (a fellow astronomer), as well as the scientific writings of Williams, Pesavento, Crawford, Meridian and so many others actively working in the burgeoning new fields of financial astrology, astro-economics and the new Money Astrology.

TREND #3
THE POWER OF SCIENCE & TECHNOLOGY

The 3rd Force Reshaping Modern Astrology Is
MODERN SCIENCE, TECHNOLOGY & THE COMPUTER
20TH CENTURY ASTROLOGY BECOMES A SCIENCE
Statistical Research, Dr. Michel Gauquelin & The Computer

THE BOTTOM-LINE: Throughout history, astrology has been more of an intuitive art than a scientific discipline. However, with the rapid advances of modern science in the 20th century, astrologers were forced to either discover a new scientific basis for astrology or get shunted into small sections on the comics pages of local newspapers. Armed with the computer, a new generation of astrologers has risen to the task with statistical research on the validity of astrological theories and practices.

Historically, we know that astrology originated about 6,000 years ago - virtually simultaneously - in three *separate* cultures, although the development of each was grounded in very similar astrological principles. J.P. Morgan's strong interest in astrology and other occult traditions drove him to dig deeper into these roots, hoping to give them a more grounded foundation.

Morgan's astrologer Evangeline Adams writes that in his "last years, he asked me from Egypt to join him and his party in the Orient, where he had gone on his famous yacht, the *Corsair*. His idea was to spend several months in a *scientific investigation* of the occult in those parts of the world where its practice reaches back to prehistoric times."

Adams declined, preferring to "pursue my own investigations, here in this little room, into the *mysteries of the human soul*." She was a psychologist at heart, on an inner journey, not a world traveller on a scientific expedition.

It wasn't until the 1970's that the scientific method overtook the field of astrology and began a massive revolution. However, the stage had been set earlier, by W. D. Gann who applied a very scientific and mathematical discipline to his research on cycles of the stock and commodities markets, and also by a government economist, Edward Dewey.

THE NEW STUDY OF CYCLES: 4,300 NATURAL & BUSINESS CYCLES

Throughout the 20th Century the United States scientific community has had considerable skepticism toward astrology. With the Great Depression that followed the stock market crash of 1929, there was an equally strong skepticism of the professional economists and market research analysts.

Edward Dewey, joined the U.S. Department of Commerce around the time of the crash and later became Chief Economist of the Department. He was the driving force behind an effort to create a more solid statistical basis on business cycles and therefore minimize the impact of future depressions. In his classic, *Cycles, The Mysterious Forces That Trigger Events,* which he co-authored with Og Mandino, the Editor of *Success* magazine, Dewey said:

"Economists disagreeing as radically as they did, I lost faith in economists, for none of them knew the answer.

"Then one day I met a man who *knew* he didn't know the answer, Chapin Hoskins, the Managing Editor of *Forbes*. He too had despaired of learning from economists why depressions happen. But he reasoned that if he couldn't discover 'why,' perhaps he could at least learn 'how.' He began to study the *behavior* of prices, production, and other measures of economic activity." He discovered cycles.

Dewey created the Foundation for the Study of Cycles, located in Wayne, Pennsylvania, after leaving the government. The Foundation has a wealth of comparative data on the cyclical patterns in many fields, economics, stock prices and bankruptcies, as well as sunspots, rainfall, wars, agricultural production, real estate sales, crime, air traffic, church membership, heart disease, brain waves, and much more. *A data base of 4,300 cycles!*

> **MONEY TOOL:** At some point you should read Dewey's book, *Cycles*, "Thus we have a synchronicity of turning points ... we were able to make comparative cycle studies that showed that substantially all the cycles of any given length turn at about the same time [therefore] it is simply inconceivable that *all* the observed coincidences could come about as a result of random forces." With these tools for scientific prediction, you can create money-making opportunities.

The really fascinating part about their research is that many of the cycles, though quite diverse, follow similar patterns (such as the 18.2 year Brenner's real estate cycle that is shared by immigrations, marriages, flood stages and the growth of some trees!). Taken as a whole they increase your ability to predict future events in advance, and profit on these new opportunities.

You'll find more about forecasting and cycles research in the discussions on Rules Two and Three.

Research in a similar vein was being conducted by communications companies beginning in the 1920's, as summarized in Lt.Cmdr. David Williams, an electrical engineer with the Consolidated Edison Company. In his books, *Financial Astrology,* and *Astro-Economics,* Williams writes of the effects of sunspot and other interplanetary activities on magnetic storms, radio transmissions, high voltage electrical power systems, blackouts, submarine activities, suicides and health problems, and many other human events.

William's two books are especially fascinating because they are also a history of the *hundreds* of individuals and organizations involved in this scientific research on astronomy and astrology in the late 19th and the 20th Century.

JUNG CHALLENGES ASTROLOGERS TO BECOME MORE SCIENTIFIC

About the same time, during the Great Depression, the psychologist Carl Jung was also nudging astrologers to become more scientific. Although Jung was a master astrologer, he was very critical of astrology's lack of a scientific grounding, noting in a 1932 lecture that "astrology would be a large scale example of synchronicity, *if it had at its disposal thoroughly tested findings.*"

Data overload is a problem, however. As the futurist, Alvin Toffler, would say about our interest in scientific data accumulation, we are in danger of being overwhelmed by this information age. Still, I believe this is a healthy environment, for now we do have a more solid scientific, statistical base for predicting the future, and this interest has provided a very positive backdrop for 20th Century developments in science of astrology.

THE POWER OF SCIENCE & TECHNOLOGY

DR. MICHEL GAUQUELIN ANSWER'S JUNG'S CHALLENGE

It wasn't until 1950 after the Second World War that a young French scientist rose to the occasion and accepted Jung's critical challenge. Dr. Michel Gauquelin, a graduate of the University of Paris with doctorates in statistics and psychology originally set out to debunk astrology. However, his life's work, until his death in 1991, proved to be a major credit to Jung's demand for a scientific basis.

Between 1950 and 1991, Dr. Gauquelin conducted numerous scientific correlation studies of more than 500,000 men and women. He investigated successful leaders in many fields, including doctors, soldiers, politicians, athletes, artists, scientists and writers. His work was made possible because Europeans allow *public* access to birth data, a definite limitation in America.

THE SUCCESS POTENTIALS of YOUR CAREER

You might ask, does your new partner or key executive have a success profile? Maybe astrology can work with your psyche tests. Gauquelin discovered statistically significant patterns for five of the key planets, Saturn, Jupiter, Mars, Venus and the Moon, although he found no statistical significance for the Sun and Mercury, nor for the slow-moving outer planets, Uranus (84 years around the Sun), Neptune (175 years) and Pluto (248).

Gauquelin's research shows a higher incidence of certain professions and business types, when the five key planets are close to one of two key axes, either your:

. **NORTH-SOUTH AXIS** near the top or the bottom, reflecting a successful life in the public eye, your career, or your

. **EAST-WEST AXIS**, especially on the left of your chart near the Ascendent, which is your relationship axis, reflecting how you are seen and what you see in others, in one-to-one relationships. The Ascendant is your projected personality, your mask, or how people view you, how you relate.

One end result of Gauquelin's research was his discovery that these certain planets frequently appeared near these main N/S and E/W axes in the following professions, and expressing certain personality traits, noted in his book, *Written In The Stars*. A few of those traits are noted here along with the planets and their respective career types:

MARS: THE EXECUTIVES, SURGEONS, MILITARY AND ATHLETES; dynamic, energetic, combative, brave, stormy, tireless, tough, reckless, daring, active, fearless, fighter, offensive, lively.

SATURN: THE RESEARCH SCIENTISTS AND PHYSICIANS; wise, methodical, thoughtful, concentrated, meticulous, introverted, precise, stiff, cold, introspective, discreet, observant.

JUPITER: THE POLITICIANS, ADVENTURERS AND ACTORS; ambitious, authoritarian, independent, proud, show off, talkative, witty, prodigal, sociable, worldly, traveller, conceited, ironical.

VENUS & MOON: THE ARTISTS, MUSICIANS AND WRITERS; creative, imaginative, poetic, spontaneous, dreamers, juvenile, seductive, friendly, agreeable, charming, generous, impressionable, attractive, easy-going, ambiguous.

The effects of the other planets on personality and career choices were not found to be statistically significant in Gauquelin's research.

Dr. Gauguelin's work did refute some of the theories and practices of astrologers, or rather his work did not *scientifically* confirm many commonly held astrological beliefs. For example, he found no evidence of the value of the Sun signs in career choices or success potentials. He did, however, discover and confirm many other personality and success patterns that were clearly beyond mere chance or coincidence.

Gauquelin's research on 500,000 birth charts has survived the test of various independent scientific associations in Europe and the U.S.A., including CSICOP, the Committee on the Scientific Investigation of Claims of the Paranormal, the scientific debunkers who publish *The Skeptical Inquirer.*

ASTROLOGY FINALLY JOINS THE AQUARIAN CONSPIRACY

The use of science in astrology has received a boost in the last decade with the organization of the First World Conference of Astro-Economics in 1987. This is a group of men and women who use astrology in various professional and business activities, although a large number are either securities trading on Wall Street or the astrological software publishers.

The World Conference of Astro-Economics gives a forum for astrologers which has been specifically denied for 50 years by The Foundation For The Study Of Cycles. Most of the Conference's workshops do focus on strategies for securities market - Gann, Elliot Wave, Kondratieff, Fibonacci. However, it is also clear that in increasing numbers astrologers are adding their perspective to the workings of the financial community. This is also a two-way street, with the best minds in the field of astrology now taking back this new information and perspective to their colleagues and students.

A MODERN ASTRONOMER COMMITS HERESY

One of the most intriguing scientific support for astrology recently came from Percy Seymour, a Fellow in the British Royal Astronomical Society. This was a big surprise because astronomers have kept their distance for the last century, maintaining a "Chinese Wall" between astronomy and astrology.

In reviewing Seymour's 1988 book, *The Scientific Basis of Astrology,* Omni magazine in 1990 had this to say about his research on the link between extraterrestrial events, and biological and other natural phenomena on Earth.

THE POWER OF PREDICTION: IN YOUR DNA/GENES? ... OR THE PLANETS?

"The physical agency that Seymour deduced is a magnetic signal from the cosmos, which would be amplified on magnetically disturbed days. The fetus in the womb might receive magnetic signals via its nervous system acting as antenna. In the same way a baby resembles its parents in appearance, Seymour says, it's magnetic antenna is wired up like theirs - sensitive to the same frequencies and resonances. So when the baby is ready to be born, it waits for a magnetic signal from the deciding planet to trigger the moment of birth.

"It is therefore no accident that this or that child is born with certain planets in primary positions. According to Seymour, the positions of the planets set off the magnetic signals that children are waiting to hear as their cues to enter the world. And each child responds to the signal that his genetic makeup has programmed him to receive."

In other words, *you decided when to be born* based on your DNA/genes, and the electromagnetic energies of the universe recorded your decision.

THE POWER OF SCIENCE & TECHNOLOGY

Gauquelin's research also confirms this link in his multi-generational research studies on parents and their children, noted in his book *Cosmic Clocks*.

It is encouraging to see Seymour confirming that *free will* is inherent in the synchronistic dynamics between our biogenetics and the electromagnetic forces of the universe. Seymour does not say that the planets *control* our destiny or *force* us do anything. Rather, he is saying that your own DNA/genes are the agent are making the birth decision. They are merely awaiting a signal, like the starter's gun in a track meet. *You still have to run the race.*

THE BOTTOM-LINE: ASTROLOGY IS TAKING A QUANTUM LEAP NOW!

Perhaps the single most important scientific and technological development that has advanced the science of astrology in the late 20th century has been the widespread use of the personal computer.

The computer has minimized the amount of time astrologers spend on tedious calculations and thus freed up the astrologer to spend more time on *interpretation* of the data rather than the *mathematics*. This trend has encouraged and even *forced* astrologers back to their historical roots in psychology.

The computer has also given astrologers the opportunity to scientifically test their work, as in the research of a French statistician and psychologist, Michel Gauquelin, and others who have followed his lead.

Dr. Gauquelin and Dr. Percy Seymour have made significant scientific contributions to the field of astrology, and as such they have been on the leading edge of another major force in the paradigm shift to the new Money A$trology, a drive for scientific validity and credibility.

PICKING THE "RIGHT" COMPUTER SOFTWARE.

Buying the right computer software is a crucial decision. For the psychologically-oriented astrologers, see the catalogues of the main companies listed above and in the appendix. The financial astrologers usually find their computer software elsewhere, with the exception of AIR Software and Astrolabe. The financial magazines have a variety of offerings for cycles research programs with astrological sub-systems. *Trader's World* magazine and catalogue is an excellent start. Here are a few software picks from the experts:

. **Astrolabe's *AstroAnalyst*** by Bill Meridian and Robert Hand.
. **AIR's new *Stock Market Program*** by Bill Meridian and Alphee Lavoie.
   Investment fund manager Meridian says, after completing the *AstroAnalyst* he "saw the need for a second program. This one provides some new techniques not provided in the first."
. **Bruce Gilmore's *WaveTrader*.**
   Market trader Pesavento says, "WaveTrader does more to describe the market than anything I've seen in twenty-seven years analyzing the markets." However, others who are less computer-oriented may find it *too* sophisticated.
. **Long's *Traders Astrological Almanac; Reversal Days For Stocks & Futures*** is also worth noting. Although not computer software, it is "easy to use...previous knowledge of planetary cycles is not needed to obtain maximum benefit from this book." The *Almanac* graphically pinpoints turning points in the market without a lot of astro-mumbo-jumbo. A simple way of adding astrology to your trading activities although you focus on other methods of tracking the markets.

Also see the catalogs of The Foundation for the Study of Cycles and Trader's World.

FUTURE SHOCK: COMPUTER TECHNOLOGY IS CREATING NEW OPPORTUNITIES IN ASTRO-ECONOMICS & FINANCIAL ASTROLOGY

The recent advances in the astrological sciences would not have been possible without the development and use of the computer by some very enterprising entrepreneurial astrologers.

Computers are definitely the key factor in accelerating the paradigm shift occurring in the later part of the 20th century. Since 1970, the rapid growth of computer technology has had a major impact on the scientific credibility of astrology, by freeing up professional practitioners so they can focus more time on the underlying psychological and economic interpretations rather than waste their valuable time on mundane, time-consuming numbers-crunching.

In this rapidly evolving economic state, the astrological *industry* is getting its own corporate structure, with several *hi-tech* newcomers added to the venerable standby of the industry, Llewellyn Publications. Thus, we now have several leading edge, hi-tech computer companies providing astrological software services and products in a thoroughly professional, business-like manner:

- **AIR Software**, West Hartford, CT (Meridian & Lavoie)
- **Astro Communication Services**, San Diego (Michelsen)
- **Astrolabe**, Boston, Massachusetts (Hand)
- **Astrology Services International**, NYC (Weingarten)
- **Matrix Software**, Big Rapids, Michigan (Erlewine)
- **MicroCycles**, Los Angeles (Stambler)

The cutting edge thinking of these astrologers and their business organizations has been invaluable in preparing American astrologers for the 21st Century.

We're on the leading edge of astrology's paradigm shift; or more accurately, we are at the center of its accelerating power, and like a jet breaking the sound barrier, we are experiencing *future shock*. And still, many astrologers and most of our society remain unaware of this subtle yet powerful shift. You must be aware, for the shift is here, now ... this new 21st Century astrology will be overwhelming the masses.

TREND #4
THE POWER OF HI-TECH MYTHOLOGY

The 4th Force Reshaping Modern Astrology Is
MYTHOLOGY, MOVIES, TELEVISION, A NEW SPIRITUALITY
THE MYTHIC ADVENTURES OF THE HERO & SHAMAN.

> **THE BOTTOM-LINE:** Due to the historically close connection between astrology and mythology, for a long time astrology was viewed by many as mere superstition, fantasy and illusion. Today, however, mythology is seen in a broader context, as an expression of the deeper psychological and spiritual bonds that connect all individuals with the collective unconscious, universal intelligence, or whatever you choose to call God. Thanks to the brilliant works of Joseph Campbell and his disciples in the film and television world, Lucas, Spielberg and others, the mythic connection between humans, the electromagnetic energies of the planets *and whatever's beyond our galaxies*, is gaining world-wide popularity.

One of the main developments in astrology's 20th Century paradigm shift flows naturally from Carl Jung to Joseph Campbell, then directly into the mythological works of those inventive hi-tech story-tellers, George Lucas and Steven Spielberg, the film directors of the three great masterpieces of our modern space mythology ... the *Star Wars Trilogy, E.T., the Extraterrestrial* and *Close Encounters Of The Third Kind.*

JOSEPH CAMPBELL, THE GODFATHER OF ASTROLOGY

Mythology has always been inherent part of the language and meaning of astrology. Mercury, Venus, Mars, Jupiter, Saturn, Neptune and Pluto are all gods from Greek mythology. For example, the god of war, Mars, remains a symbol of aggressive behavior, conflict, exploration, entrepreneurialism and the pioneering spirit. What's new in the 20th century is that Carl Jung's work has inspired a more systematic, more universal and more scholarly approach to mythology that has also re-anchored astrology into its mythological roots, as well as its psychological roots.

While Michel Gauquelin took up one of Carl Jung's challenges - namely Jung's criticism of the absence of scientific research on astrology - Joseph Campbell took up another significant challenge. With his monumental research on mythology and the great mythic archetypes originally identified by Jung, Campbell further anchored Jungian psychology into it's roots ... roots that are not only in astrology but also in mythology, shamanism, Zen Buddhism, the I Ching, Christian mysticism, and the Tarot. In this context, all of life is seen as one comprehensive tapestry, with all the pieces linked in one complex network.

My exposure to Joseph Campbell's stimulating genius happened quite by accident during my *midlife crisis,* while working by day in the very left-brained Wall Street world. At that time I was one of the *grey masses* racing through Manhattan, wearing three-piece suits, carrying two briefcases, and more obsessed about the next multi-million dollar investment deal than about *investing* in my personal growth and development.

My midlife crisis actually turned out to be quite profitable because I had the good fortune of being dragged by a friend to a number of new experiences. One of these was a weekly workshop on "dance meditation" that I attended for over five years in a Soho loft, hosted by Calvin Holt, the enigmatic and ebullient owner of the Serendipity Restaurant in New York City.

This workshop became so important to me that I once flew back from Texas one evening for our relatively short dance *practice,* then back to Texas at midnight, in order not to miss our group. At the time I was working on a $360 million deal, but Calvin's dance meditation group was more important.

The other stroke of good fortune was an opportunity to actually attend one of Joseph Campbell's workshops on "Mythical Meditation." To this day I vividly remember thinking to myself as we completed the workshop, "Hey, this is a historic event, why aren't there more people here?"

HOW TO MEDITATE, STUDY MYTHOLOGY & EXERCISE AT THE SAME TIME!

One of Campbell's very simple anecdotes still stands out as a special memory of that workshop. Because the workshop's title was "Mythical Meditation," it was natural that at one point someone would ask him *how he meditated.* His answer was quite telling about how the man lived and breathed his life's work. He explained how he meditated on each of the twenty-two major cards of The Tarot as he swam laps in his backyard pool, for in them was expressed "the total connection between human beings and the collective unconscious."

The impact of my meeting Campbell was immediate and powerful. I jumped into Jungian psychology, took acting and dance lessons. I bought a life-sized chrome plated mannequin in a dance pose and began writing a screenplay about her. In three months I had a 150-page romantic thriller about J.P. Morgan IV and Francesca, an Italian ballerina, Wall Street and the Mafia. Later, as I learned more about Jungian psychology, I discovered that Francesca was an archetype, my *alter ego,* my feminine half, *the woman inside every man*, the source of my creativity. Getting in touch with her allowed me to better understand my masculinity *and my inner astrologer.*

THE SUPER HI-TECH MYTHMAKERS ... LUCAS & SPIELBERG

Actually it wasn't until years later that I fully realized how important Joseph Campbell really was to the storytellers of Hollywood and the entertainment world. When I was Executive Vice President for Michael Phillips, the producer of *Close Encounters Of The Third Kind, The Sting* and *Taxi Driver,* George Lucas publicly acknowledged that Campbell's works on mythology were the creative inspiration for his *Star Wars Trilogy.* At many public tributes the last few years of his life, Campbell was recognized by thousands of other members of the film and television community for his great inspiration to the creative fields.

When Joseph Campbell appeared on a television program about George Lucas, *Myths, Magic And The Force,* Campbell remarked that, "All myths have to do with the transformation of consciousness." Indeed, that's what Campbell himself was doing all along, as a channel of the collective unconscious. For films like *Star Wars* and *Close Encounters* have had an enormous impact on many individuals, collectively energizing the paradigm shift, transforming us at a new level of the collective unconscious that binds us all.

THE POWER OF HI-TECH MYTHOLOGY

The *Star Wars* myth alone has educated and inspired *hundreds of millions* of people worldwide with its epic storytelling about the great conflicts between The Force and The Empire, good versus evil. We participated in the heroic adventures of the androgynous twin leaders, Skywalker and Princess Lea, their story reflecting our present world's struggle to survive as the millennium rapidly approaches. In their story we experienced the transformation of the human race through the influential mentoring of Yoda and Obi Wan Kanobi, as channels of *The Force* (the universal intelligence or God).

CLOSE ENCOUNTERS: STAR TREK, STARMAN & STAR WARS ... HI-TECH MYTHS ARE OPENING PEOPLE TO THE NEW ASTROLOGY

Astrology has always been closely linked to the great historical myths. In the past quarter century, however, that link has become much more powerful and more universal. Many new adventures about an exciting future in space have tapped into the collective unconsciousness of mass audiences in every continent on Earth. We saw the first signs of this new hi-tech power on television, with the classic futuristic adventure, the *Star Trek* saga.

Today, the mythological works of Carl Jung and Joseph Campbell, and the commercial story-telling of George Lucas, Stephen Spielberg and others has created a universal bond previously missing in the world. A shared mythology that cuts across every culture and into every heart, bringing with it a new era. With it comes an openness to and acceptance of astrology.

Today *Star Wars* is an expression of your individual heroic struggles played out on an epic scale in the galaxies; a true projection of the synchronistic bond between each human's genes and the electromagnetic forces of planets and the stars. The *Star Wars* myth is the new astrology in action, a powerful *projection* of the inner workings of your *inner astrologer.*

Campbell, Lucas and the others gave us a better understanding of the archetypal forces at work in our lives. They did this by helping us project the struggle outside ourselves, allowing us to see our human desire to transform and to unite with the *collective unconscious,* the divine. In the process, we are close to understanding the greater paradigm shift surrounding all of us, as we approach the end of this exciting millennium.

BOX-OFFICE SUCCESS: PSYCHOLOGY + MYTHOLOGY + A$TROLOGY

In summary, it now seems clear that, in this century, Jung, Lucas, Campbell, Roddenberry, Spielberg and many other hi-tech storytellers are all locked in an *unconscious conspiracy* that is weaving together their creative works as an expression of the seven basic archetypes that Jung says drive each individual - archetypes that are also a reflection of the larger dimensions of our humanity and of a collective unconscious linked to the galaxies and beyond to a universal intelligence.

With the large-scale acceptance of Jungian psychology in the field of astrology, mythology (both the ancient mythology of troubadour's song and fairy tales, and modern hi-tech mythology of film and television) has become a major force in the new 21st Century astrology, and with it is coming a new public acceptance of the new Money A$trology as a practical decision-making tool.

HI-TECH MYTHOLOGY: YOU ARE THE MOVIES YOU EAT!

Archetypes *pop up* all around us - in our hi-tech mythology, in the science of psychology, in television ads and movies, and in modern astrology. We often absorb multiple messages simultaneously on the many channels of our minds.

For example, I'm eating popcorn watching the STAR WARS' heros on television and on comes Orville Redenbacher encouraging me to, "Pick one thing and do it well." That message taps into my inner hero, inspiring me into action!

Discovering your archetypes is one of the best kinds of therapy. Archetypes are a reflection of your many inner selves. They are a projection of your wildest dreams. They help you get to know who you really are. They inspire you to *be all that you can be*.

There's money in discovering the power of *your* mythic archetypes.

Carl Jung says there are seven primary archetypes shared by each one of us:
- **The Self**, your higher power, the Universal, Yoda and *the Force!*
- **The Feminine**, your receptivity to relationships, Princess Lea.
- **The Masculine**, the rational and material side of life, Hans Solo.
- **The Heroic**, the drive to transform into the Self, Luke Skywalker.
- **The Adversary**, your darkside, enemies within and without, Darth Vader.
- **Death and Rebirth**, or life's dynamic, repetitive cycles.
- **The Journey**, the linear march of life's events and stages.

Within this dynamic fabric of mythology we merge with the higher forces within ourselves and we merge *into* the larger forces around us - our community, our nation, the planet and the universe.

As a result of this new mass awareness, the *new hi-tech mythology of Lucas and Spielberg is rapidly creating the new reality - the new paradigm* - and paving the way of the emerging new astrology of the 21st Century.

TREND #5
THE POWER OF CREATIVE ACTION

The 5th Force Reshaping Modern Astrology Is
A CREATIVE "WHACK ON THE SIDE OF THE HEAD"
WHERE YOU ARE YOUR OWN BEST ASTROLOGER!
Searching For The Future Amid Uncertainty & Chaos.

> **THE BOTTOM-LINE:** Today most enlightened individuals have discarded the belief that astrology is some dark, external force determining and controlling future events. Instead, leading-edge thinkers now see astrology as a positive tool that is within their control. It is a "whack on the side of the head," kicking them out of their old thinking habits and ruts, a method of opening their minds to new ideas and new solutions, a way of releasing the powers already hidden deep within their psyches!

Shortly after meeting Joseph Campbell, I had my first big lesson on how astrology and astrologers can unlock our hidden dreams. When a psychologist I met at his workshop encouraged me to see an astrologer I laughed, "Not me, that's for *Ladies Home Journal* readers." It was nine months before I got the courage to follow her advice, and even then I felt that I was "cheating" on the tough-minded world of investment banking. Finally, curiosity won out.

MAKING A QUANTUM LEAP FROM WALL STREET TO HOLLYWOOD

"You should have been making musical comedies on the stage, or in film and television, definitely something in the creative arts." I laughed when Julie Bresciani, my first astrologer, made that comment about five minutes into my first meeting with her. At the time I was forty, right in the middle of my midlife crisis.

"Come on, Julie, I'll bet you say that to every up-tight investment banker who comes in wearing a three-piece suit. You just want us to feel good."

"Not so, here I'll show you." She was convincing as she zipped through my chart's interpretation. Julie was a psychology teacher at Marymount college and an astrologer. My flippant manner changed to intense curiosity as she elaborated on the creative nature of my chart.

Perhaps I shouldn't have been surprised as I had written and starred in a senior class play in high school and had enrolled in art teachers college in Pennsylvania before joining the Marine Corps. But then my creativity went "underground." Or into business projects, rather than the "pure" artistry that excited me in high school. Film-making *never* occurred to me.

> **SUCCESS FACT:** Within 40 days after my first astrologer's advice, I wrote a thirty-page screenplay treatment. Within six months I had a 150 page script. A year later I won a gold medal for a short film I directed. The following year I wrote a 140 page script for a musical comedy based on Goethe's *Faust*. And less than ten years later, I was head of the Financial News Network, a national cable channel and Executive Vice President of Mercury Entertainment Corporation. I also wrote a couple feature film scripts and directed and produced an hour-long documentary about the midlife crisis period, titled *Modern Man In Search Of His Soul, Conversations With The Transforming Man*.

All this happened because Joseph Campbell got me to an astrologer who then told me I should have been working on projects for film, television and the stage. It sounded like a fun idea, so I did it. It was an idea waiting to happen.

For me astrology works!

ROGER VON OECH'S WACKY, NUTTY CREATIVITY

Actually my first clue about this *creativity* force reshaping astrology came from reading Roger von Oech's books, *A Whack On The Side Of The Head,* and *A Kick In The Seat Of The Pants.* Dr. von Oech has a doctorate from Stanford University in management sciences. He is also President of "Creative Think," a management consulting and training firm that stimulates creativity and innovation in business, working for such clients as IBM, NBC, NASA and Xerox.

"The title of this book," begins Roger von Oech, author of *A Kick In The Seat Of The Pants,* "like that of it's predecessor," *A Whack On The Side Of The Head,* "reflects my basic belief that once a person settles into a comfortable routine, he needs extraordinary measures to get him up and say, 'I'm going to try something different.'" So, he uses comedy, artistic sketching, magic and many other random and unexpected techniques to unlock and awaken the creative spirit within you. Roger von Oech's creativity flows through a 4-step process:
1. **Explorer** - searching for new ideas outside you
2. **Artist** - your intuition playing with new ideas from within
3. **Judge** - a hard look at the bottom-line and a decision
4. **Warrior** - into action with the killer instinct

Everyone could use *a whack on the side of the head* sometime in their life, to wake up their creativity, no matter what business they're in.

Similarly, the profession of astrology could use an infusion of creative fun. Many astrologers treat astrology as a deadly serious business drained of any creative spark. They often tend to focus too heavily on the darkside and the negative rather than the opportunities. That's why I believe most traditional astrologers, *as well as their clients,* could use a whack on the side of the head, a tap on the funny bone; and a shot of positive thinking!

LAUGH & SET FREE THE CREATIVE GIANT WITHIN

Experiment! Let the creative astrologer within you loose on an adventure for a few minutes, or hours, or a weekend of creativity ... you just might trip over a few unexpected new ideas, maybe even discover one or two incredibly new solutions to nagging, old problems.

Meditate on one of your chart's interpretations. Write about your goals for the next few hours. Do it in conjunction with the goal-setting approach used in Tony Robbins' *Awaken The Giant Within.* Share it with a friend. Be open to surprises. *Expect the unexpected and it will happen.* Astrology should be enjoyable, while creating prosperity and wealth for you. Let yourself go!

MONEY TIP: HIRE YOUR OWN CORPORATE ASTROLOGER!
Many executives preparing their quarterly and annual forecasts will review all kinds of "very serious" materials, economic, trade and financial reports, newsletters, *Forbes, Business Week* and *The Wall Street Journal.* They'll talk to their attorneys, accountants, economists and mentors, and they'll get planning information from many, many other resources.

Why not introduce some real creativity and do something totally bizarre ... hire a corporate astrologer! And if public opinion worries you, give the astrologer a good *cover* - a mainstream, respectable title like *strategic cycles analyst.*

THE POWER OF CREATIVE ACTION

I've know many hard-nosed business and financial types that respond well to astrology because it can be an easy, fun way of releasing creative energies, and in the process revealing valuable new facts, ideas and directions.

Consult your astrologer for a totally different perspective, call it a "second opinion" much in the same vein as the ancient kings consulted their court jester. Maybe, just maybe, you'll discover one or more new solutions to a major production problem, or an investment opportunity. Or you'll discover a new market for your product, or a new area of expansion!

Whatever works for you. Be adventurous. Experiment with the new Money Astrology. Then try the Whack Pack, the Tarot, I Ching, Runes, psychics, even a "random walk" in the Smart Yellow Pages ... *whatever works to give you that crucial whack on the side of the head.*

And remember, you're in good company, with J. Pierpont Morgan, Carl Jung, Franklin D. Roosevelt, Ronald Reagan, a few good presidents of the New York Stock Exchange, and many more leaders.

FREE WILL: THE PSYCHE *IS* THE COSMOS, YOU CONTROL THE STARS

Many traditionalists fear astrology because they believe, erroneously, that astrology is deterministic, that the planets control human decision-making, eliminating all possibility of creative free will.

The new paradigm is based on a radically different perspective ... that astrology is a simply a roadmap, suggesting potential paths and signposts in life. *Nothing is predetermined.*

Every human remains in the driver's seat, still in control of their decisions, and still totally responsible for the results, the good, the bad and the ugly!

For many, creativity is a lost part of their soul. Their creativity has been overwhelmed by the left-brain, and dominated by a project-oriented, rational-thinking, solutions-focused, work-a-day world that demands practical results. It is this urge to create that is fueling the paradigm shift into the 21st Century. It is a struggle between the need to create anew versus the stagnation of the old paradigm. Today this new astrology has become a major new tool that can help you tap into the creative genius within you.

DISCOVERING YOUR "INNER ASTROLOGER"

This astrology of creative decision-making, the new Money Astrology, reflects the new paradigm, where *you are your own best astrologer,* intuitively and without further analysis. It is based on Jung's *synchronicity,* the connection between your body's genes and electromagnetic energies of the planetary, where *the psyche is the cosmos.*

You and your DNA/genes are *always* the best possible judge of your destiny ... *if* you just listen to your inner creative voice, and trust your *inner astrologer.*

This is the essence of creative or intuitive astrology ... an inner conviction.

In his 1948 classic, *This Thing Called You,* Ernest Holmes, the founder of Science of Mind, observed that, "Not only humans, but everything in nature is endowed with this creative urge ... it is impossible to escape."

Men and women alike have this basic urge to create somewhere. To make something that's never been done. To express the deepest most recesses of their soul. To echo their inner most voices, the spirit of God within them, and the darkest shadows of their past. To create that which did not exist before they walked this earth. To rise to your highest potentials in this life. To become *this thing called you!"*

The new astrology will help you set free this *creative power.*

> **DANGER: NEW TERMS AHEAD ... DISCOVER A NEW FUTURE!**
>
> Yes, you will be exposed to some buzzwords, or rather, a new technical language. It can't be avoided. But I've tried to keep the jargon to an absolute minimum, and keep it as simple as possible for you.
>
> Just bear with me, because it's worth it.
>
> My goal for the remainder of this book is not - *I repeat not* - to make you an *expert* astrologer. I really don't even expect you to learn much of the language that I use, *because you don't need it to succeed with this new astrology!*
>
> I know that if you're like most successful people in the business and financial world, you'll *"tune-out"* if you see too many astrological symbols or hear too much stuff about Uranus, Ascendants, Moon phases, Sextiles, retrogrades, etc.
>
> *It's natural to tune-out new stuff!*
>
> If you don't grasp the details on your first reading, don't worry, *it's probably not essential!*
>
> It's far more important for you to get a sense of the *bigger picture.*
>
> My goal in this book is quite simple: I want you to *get a feel of* the many potential uses of astrology and it's credibility in the practical world of business and finance.
>
> *Why?* Because Money A$trology is a powerful tool that's already helping many successful men and women make profitable decisions ... today!

PART TWO: HOW IT WORKS

"The Rules of The Game"

SUCCESSFUL DECISION-MAKING using THE SEVEN RULES OF MONEY A$TROLOGY

PART TWO: HOW IT WORKS

A$TROLOGY for SUCCESSFUL DECISION-MAKING
Power Formula: The Rules Of The Game

AN OVERVIEW of THE SEVEN RULES of MONEY A$TROLOGY

Before we get into the details of the seven key rules of the new astrology in the next seven sections of this book, let's take a moment for an overview of these seven rules for successful decision-making, the *power formula* for the emerging new Money A$trology.

You're reading this because you want to know how the new astrology can help *you* maximize your financial power, minimize your economic risks *and* achieve true freedom and security. How can you use astrology when you're expanding a business or investing in a major real estate deal, or coping with a major life-cycle or career transition, or just trying to manage a tight bank account in a unpredictable economic environment?

There are *seven key rules* essential to using astrology effectively with money, business and financial decision-making. Follow these simple rules and you will discover new levels of success and prosperity in all areas of your life ... financial and economic, psychological and spiritual.

> **RULE #1.** **FOCUS ON THE RIGHT TARGET; MAKE SURE YOUR BUSINESS & CAREER DECISIONS POINT IN THE RIGHT DIRECTION,** That You Are Following Your Bliss, Your Dreams, Your Destiny, Your Vision, Your Life's Mission ... And Not Someone Else's!

The phrase, "do what you love and the money will follow," captures the spirit here. Like a Air Force test pilot, if you're headed for the right target, you're more likely to score a hit and win at the money game.

Most people never achieve their highest potentials because they're "off-track." Campbell would say they're not *following their bliss*. If you're focused on the right target, financial success is not only more likely, it *will* reflect your inner spiritual prosperity.

The new astrology can help you define your goals or life mission and avoid running up financial dead-ends. To begin with, forget everything you know about the popular *Sun sign* astrology. Those gross generalizations written for twenty-one million Americans born under each of the twelve signs are usually inaccurate and misleading.

The house positions of *your* Moon, Venus, Mars, Jupiter and Saturn, the signs ruling *your* Midheaven and Ascendant, and so many other factors are far more important to your economic success than your Sun sign!

You are a totally unique individual, one-of-a-kind. Your astrological profile is as complex as the chromosome structure of your DNA/genes. You are a complex network of *thousands* of interactions between the ten key planets, their signs and aspects, their house placements, etc.

If astrological research studies show major differences between twins born just minutes apart, you can bet you'll have little in common with millions of other Americans merely because they're born under your Sun sign.

Don't surrender your unique identity to the masses. Look for the key astrological themes that distinguish your success profile. Search for your special mission in life. Discover what makes you unique. Make sure that you are locked on *your* target!

> **RULE #2. LEARN TO PREDICT THE BEST TIME FOR YOUR DECISIONS; Know Your Power Days, The Challenges As Well As The Opportunities, Then Go For It, Be A Winner!**

Build a winning game plan around an understanding of your psychological life-cycles. These can be identified astrologically by looking at the houses transited by the major planets over the next few years.

The powerful influence of Saturn and Jupiter house *transits* has been scientifically identified by several astrologer-psychologists, notably Robert Hand and Stephen Arroyo. For example, we know that Jupiter transits of the ninth house will trigger a fundamental shift in your basic philosophy of life, while Saturn in your third house can restructure your way of thinking logically and communicating in business.

Certain planetary transits are also tied to the major psychological life-cycles and personal transitions. As a result, you may instinctively understand your life mission and still be full of doubts, because a difficult life-cycle is creating major obstacles and obscuring your vision. *The secret* is in working *with* your cycles rather than abandoning your dreams.

> **RULE #3. LEARN TO PREDICT YOUR COMPETITION'S FUTURE BEHAVIOR IN THE MARKETPLACE: Use Mass Psychology & The Astrological Transits To Profit on Your Competition's Next Moves.**

Here's the only area where the Sun sign astrology may work in your favor. Since millions of Americans are still influenced by their daily Sun sign horoscopes based on the general transits. These few simple steps can help you *psych-out* the players and win the money game, whether you're pitted against the general business public, the stock market or an individual adversary or partner.

In brief, let *them* follow their Sun signs, while *you follow your chart.* Plan *your* decisions based on *your* unique chart and transits. Next, analyze the general daily transits to predict the conventional wisdom of the masses. Then, *always* make final decisions based on your own chart data, using the mass data to confirm whether "they" are moving *with you* (opportunities), or *against you* (challenges). *Never* follow the herd. Even when it's headed your way, lead the pack.

> **RULE #4. LEVERAGE YOUR POWER BY PICKING WITH THE RIGHT TEAM, RIGHT PARTNERS, RIGHT RELATIONSHIPS & RIGHT NETWORK, Create A Balance of Power with a Positive Support System.**

Success with money often depends on leveraging your resources. You can increase your economic power by surrounding yourself with the right people ... the right business partners, attorneys, bankers, doctors, therapists, mentors, stockbrokers, gurus, friends, and your mate. They are your team. They are the *power behind the throne.*

PART TWO: HOW MODERN ASTROLOGY WORKS 43

Astrological compatibility studies can help you evaluate the success potentials of a relationship, intimates or business partners. First, separately study the charts of each person. Then, their compatibilities are analyzed to determine the opportunities and challenges facing the relationship, by comparing the signs and house positions of the Sun, Moon, Venus, Mars and Ascendant or your Rising Sign. Compatibility studies can maximize chances of a profitable relationship, before *investing* your valuable time and money.

> **RULE #5.** **LOCATE YOUR BEST GEOGRAPHIC POWER BASE;** Then Make A Power Move. Either Relocate There ... Or Capitalize On The Inherent Power Of Your Existing Location.

You may be playing the money game in the wrong stadium. If you are, your current geographic location could be a liability to your financial success. Astro*Carto*Graphy and other kinds astro-locality studies are a new branch of astrology, developed in recent years to help you analyze the best places for you to live and work.

By moving to a new location, or by selecting the right market location for you and your organization, it's possible to shift planets into your chart's powerhouses and you may increase your chances of success. For example, moving to New Mexico may favor the arts for you, while New York City may support real estate development projects (or visa versa). You can also use these techniques to double-check travel plans as well as your relocations decisions. You'll see how these work in detail in a later section.

Just remember, *every* location has its unique pros and cons. So, whatever your decision, no matter what economic arena you finally pick, stay or go, own your choice 100%! Then *play hard, and plan to win!*

> **RULE #6.** **ALWAYS GET A SECOND OPINION TO MINIMIZE YOUR RISKS & MAXIMIZE YOUR OPPORTUNITIES FOR SUCCESS;** Always, No Matter What Your Issues Or Who Your Experts!

After the initial interpretation of your chart and cycles, your decisions can be double-checked using *proven astrological techniques.* For example, *horary* charting can forecast answers to any questions, including money decisions. And *electional* techniques will help you select critical dates, such as the right time to begin a new business venture or apply for a loan. In each case a chart is cast to *create the birth moment* of the question, an event or a decision.

In general, no one should ever rely solely on the advice of any one expert, whether an accountant, attorney, astrologer, or doctor, regardless of their reputation. Always get a second opinion from another trusted advisor, no matter what the question, no matter who the advisor. *Always.*

> **RULE #7.** **JUST DO IT - GET INTO ACTION WITH TOTAL COMMITMENT TO YOUR GAMEPLAN, THEN ...** And Stay In The Game, No Matter What; Don't Quit 5 Minutes Before The Miracle Happens!

Tenacity is the single biggest key to success. Many new ventures have the vision, yet fail when the going gets tough. Rediscover this powerful message resonating in Napoleon Hill's inspirational classic, *Think and Grow Rich.* Winners don't quit.

The psychologist Dr. Carl G. Jung was a master astrologer. His concept of synchronicity links together:
- your DNA-genes, the inner you, with the
- electromagnetic energies of the planets *out there*.

Your chart was imprinted on your blood cells at birth. Your chart is like a computer memory chip. You instinctively act in sync with the planets.

You are your own best astrologer.
Trust your instincts.
Set your goals high.
Then shift into action and *expect to succeed*.
Go for it!
Don't quit five minutes before the miracle happens.
By following these seven rules, you can *make the miracles happen for you!*

**WHAT CAN YOU EXPECT IN THE NEXT 7 CHAPTERS?
DETAILS ON THE 7 RULES OF MONEY A$TROLOGY.**

In the next seven chapters you will be looking at the details on how these Seven Rules of Money A$trology are already being used by traders, investors, entrepreneurs and business executives to make decisions and make money.
BUT BEFORE YOU GO ANY FURTHER, TAKE A PEEK AT APPENDIX FOUR.
Although I know that someone like you who is focusing primarily on financial astrology and astro-economics may not be interested in the same kinds of astronomic data as the personal astrologers, I also know that eventually you will need some basic background in the new astrological analysis, which is included in the next two chapters on Rules One and Two.
In addition, I strongly suggest that you review the *related* information in Appendix Four. It includes: a "Mini-Crash Course" in Astrology, an Astrological Profile Analysis, "Zip-Code" Interpretations of basic astrological terms, and the "10 Personality Profiles for Business Success." You need to be aware of these resources when you're reading the next 7 chapters about the 7 key rules for successful decision-making.

The Astrology Of Successful Decision-Making

1. TARGETING THE RIGHT MISSION & GOALS

> **SUCCESS RULE #1.**
> **FOCUS ON THE RIGHT TARGET; MAKE SURE YOUR BUSINESS & CAREER DECISIONS ARE POINTED IN THE RIGHT DIRECTION,** That You Are Following Your Bliss, Your Dreams, Your Destiny, Your Vision, Your Life's Mission ... And Not Someone Else's!

When J. Pierpont Morgan first visited his astrologer he wasn't a bank clerk looking for a few winning lotto numbers.

Morgan came first class, in a carriage, wearing a tophat and tailored waistcoat, driven from his mansion in uptown Manhattan to the Windsor Hotel by a chauffeur, protected by a bodyguard.

Most people would say, this man certainly needs no help from an astrologer.

The Morgans were already one of the richest and most powerful financial dynasties in the entire world. The House of Morgan had financed the Civil War and the making of U.S. Steel, to mention a few of their accomplishments.

Why then does a billionaire with a virtual monopoly on American business and international finance seek out the advice of an astrologer.

Why? He wanted an edge! Morgan wanted an edge on his competition. He wanted to keep the winner's edge he already had, and he wanted more. He wanted to live life to the fullest. He wanted to *live on that edge!* Like an test pilot, he was *pushing the envelope* to its limits!

Actually, Morgan *was* seeking a few winning lotto numbers! That's why the cocky Morgan later said, "millionaires don't hire astrologers, billionaires do!"

YOUR BIGGEST CHALLENGE ... KNOWING WHO YOU ARE

Before his visit, Morgan sent his secretary ahead with his birth data in a sealed envelop, so that Evangeline Adams could save him time and calculate his birth chart before he arrived.

Astrologers, like accountants, need time to "crunch the numbers" and "work up the figures" before the client walks in. More importantly, they need time to *interpret* the basic data. They must answer the question, what does it all mean?

As the great Carl Jung said, "The fact that it is possible to construct, in adequate fashion, a person's character from the date of his nativity, shows the relative validity of astrology. Whatever is born or done this moment, has the qualities of this moment in time."

> **YOUR BUSINESS, CAREER & FINANCIAL DECISIONS**
> If astrology worked for J.P. Morgan, it can work for you too. You can also learn how to "think astrology & grow rich" ... how can astrology help you make decisions, regardless of whether it's a major decision on:
> . strategies for expanding a multi-million dollar business,
> . taking a job offer that's not on your career path,
> . making a major purchase of some production equipment,
> . deciding on one or more new investment opportunities,
> . entering into a marriage or a business partnership,
> . signing important contracts or loan agreements, and other decisions.

Other decisions are equally important ... like marketing a new product line, or picking the best dates for a presentation, or determining when to deliver important messages, or buying a new home, or making travel arrangements, or perhaps even a decision like what to wear at a public event, especially if you want to project confidence and be seen as a winner.

Please do not misunderstand me. I am *not* suggesting you run off and consult with your astrologer *before* you make *every* decision. That would be nonsense. In fact, ultimately you may want to talk to an astrologer *only* during major crises, for a second opinion, assuming you are in touch with your own center, your own *inner astrologer.*

SUCCESSFUL DECISION-MAKING: "KNOW THYSELF" FIRST

What I am emphasizing is that your best decisions will be made when *you first "know thyself."* Sound advice that Plato gave his followers many centuries ago. His advice has been repeated many times throughout history, most recently during the 20th century paradigm shift, by a number of motivational leaders and success coaches, each in their own way:

Napoleon Hill; success will come because you have a *definiteness of purpose* and a *burning desire* driving your actions, never give up. **Anthony Robbins**; *awaken the giant within you,* take control of your life and achieve *peak performance,* shape your destiny, you are the master of your own fate, the captain of your ship, and *live with passion.* **Les Brown**; *live your dreams,* find out what it is you want out of your life, and go after it as if your life depends on it. Why? Because it does! **Robert Schuller**; *be an extraordinary person in an ordinary world,* think possibilities and achieve the impossible. **Joseph Campbell**; *follow your bliss,* no matter what.

In fact, virtually every book I've ever read on success motivation, business management and career planning has a section on goal-setting and the preparation of a mission statement for you and your organization.

Who are you? What is your destiny in life? The question is often asked. Yet many people ignore the question, and need occasional reminders.

The amount of advice is endless, just look in any major bookstore, especially in the self-help section. The *starting point* is always the same, "know thyself." Come from your own center. Be true to *your destiny.* Or pay the consequences. For example, "If you don't know who you are, the stock market is an expensive place to find out," cautions Adam Smith in *The Money Game*.

Where astrology comes in. Astrology is primarily a decision-making tool, one of many in the computer *powerbooks* of successful men and women in the world of business and finance. It can help you understand how to make the best possible decisions by helping you better understand who you are, your personality and your goals.

SUCCESS TIP: IF YOU ARE IN TOUCH WITH YOUR INNER ASTROLOGER, YOU ALREADY KNOW YOUR MISSION AND YOUR GOALS!

The main purpose of natal astrology is to help you get in touch with your inner self, for you are your own best astrologer, the source of your power. Astrology and astrologers cannot to make decisions for you. In the final analysis, you remain the ultimate decision-maker, guided by your inner astrologer.

If you are in close contact with your inner astrologer, then you already know your destiny and your goals. In that case you don't need astrology to help you *set goals*, rather you will use it to help you make decisions during major personal life crises and business turning points, as discussed in Rules 2 & 3.

TARGETING THE RIGHT GOALS 47

> **CAREER GOALS: INVESTMENT BANKER, PROMOTER OR POLITICIAN?**
> An investment banker came to me for a consultation about his business activities. We talked about his planned acquisition of a small bank. I told him that he had a super-strong signature of a politician as well as a financial leader. He ignored my comments and we continued discussing the bank deal. After I brought up his mission as a politician for the fifth time he finally said, "You're right. Now you and my mother know it, my secret passion for politics. But I won't do it until I have a personal fortune to back me. Just keep this quiet."
> Today he is on the way to achieving his financial goals.

KNOW YOUR MISSION, TARGET YOUR GOALS

If you're headed for a target you're more likely to score a hit. Let's face it, *you can't hit your target if you don't know where it is.* That's sound advice whether you are piloting a 747 to Hong Kong, quarterbacking a Superbowl game, or negotiating on an offer to invest in a real estate partnership.

Focusing on the right target is another way of telling you that you *must* do some *goal-setting. You must define your personal goals.* Or, if you're writing a business plan for your new company's presentation to a bank or a group of investors, you need a *mission statement.*

> **A GLOBAL EXAMPLE of THE POWER OF A MISSION**
> Even the Japanese and other Asian cultures - strong believers in the Judo, of flowing with the natural forces of nature - have very focused mission statements guiding their business decisions. I remember it was only a short time ago in 1974, when the Japanese Minister of Finance began giving permission for Japanese companies to invest in U.S. real estate.
> I was at Morgan Stanley when Mitsubishi International asked us to advise them on the strange ways of our nation's investment habits. Their team was headed by a former Zero pilot who shot down 19 U.S. aircraft, and was staffed by a young kid out of engineering school, a middle manager from the Mitsubishi oil tanker chartering business, and another young man whose father was a comic and mother was a Zen priestess. They were a motley crew indeed.
> But they had a mission! Buy American real estate, lots of it. In 1974 New York University's *Real Estate Review* published my article, "Strategies For Foreign Corporations in U.S. Realty," where I estimated that *total* U.S. real estate in the hands of foreign owners amounted to only $5 billion. A short 15 years later, the Japanese had advanced so fast they were buying over $10 billion in American real estate *annually* in the late 1980's.

Now *that* shows the power of a mission!

Know thyself. Set goals. Yours. Follow your bliss, your vision. Live your dreams, your destiny. Discover your mission in life. Be all you can be.

Focus on the right target ... your target. Lock on it.

SIX WARNINGS: *BEFORE* YOU USE THE NEW A$TROLOGY

How can astrologers help you *think astrology and grow rich*? First of all, please remember that new astrology need not be as complicated as many books on astrology may lead you to believe. Of course the insiders and high priests of any organization will create a mystique, but the basics are relatively simple if you keep in mind these six warnings:

FIRST: NEW ASTROLOGY FOCUSES ON YOUR HOUSES, NOT SIGNS!
Dr. Gauquelin's scientific research found *no statistical validity* in the *signs* of the planets, but in the 500,000 charts studied he did discover considerable research data to support the importance of the positions of the planets near the main axes in certain Houses, which will be discussed further as we go on.

SECOND: THE MYTH OF THE SUN SIGN'S IMPORTANCE.
Even if you are using the signs, the Sun is only one source of electromagnetic energy out there, and it is certainly not the most important one in an astrologer's analysis and interpretations. While Dr. Gauquelin's research studies suggested that the *signs of all planets* were statistically insignificant compared to the house position of the planets, the signs do become important in two areas; (a) the signs on the axes, that is, the Rising sign and the Midheaven's sign, and (b) the dominant signs of the planets as a whole, *i.e., the elements*, which are discussed in detail below.

THIRD: IGNORE THE MORE ESOTERIC ASTRONOMIC FACTS.
Many astrologers would like you to believe stuff like moon wobbles are significant enough to control and override the major decisions of your life. Every profession had their in-group jargon, most of which accounts for less than 10% of the total analysis, including progressions, asteroids, house rulers, retrogrades, interceptions, moon wobbles, and other fancier hocus-pocus and mumbo-jumbo. I suggest you ignore them for now, or ask an expert.

FOURTH: FOR NOW, PUT ASIDE THE FANCY ASTRO-TECHNIQUES.
Including the partnership and compatibility studies, relocation studies, horary and electional techniques, mundane and political astrology, and corporate chart analyses. Put them aside *until* you first identify *your* mission, *your* goals and the astrological life-cycle you are in. None of those extra astrological techniques are of any value to you unless and until you *first* analyze your natal chart, to identify your mission and develop a set of life goals.

FIFTH: NEVER LET AN ASTROLOGER MAKE YOUR DECISIONS.
Unfortunately, many clients make gurus out of their astrologers, creating an advisor who can do no wrong. Luckily, however, the sharper clients are usually working on their goals through other avenues and just want a second opinion or sounding board. For example, one used Anthony Robbins' *Personal Power* tapes while on a vacation in Tahiti, another attended a career planning workshop at the Big Sur's Esalen Institute, another was doing the work while preparing his corporation's new business plan, and using *Success* magazine's *BizPlan* software. You should every possible resource available.

SIXTH: REMEMBER, YOU ARE YOUR OWN BEST ASTROLOGER.
Jung's concept of synchronicity tells me that you really are your own best astrologer. Let's face it, ultimately you're stuck with the responsibility for all your decisions anyway, and you *must* make every one of them, consciously or by default. You had better feel passionate about your mission, and you better set some goals!
Your decisions can never really be delegated to an astrologer, an attorney, an accountant, or your father. In the end, the responsibility is totally yours. Learn to *listen to the voice within you.* Your astrologer can help, but what does your *inner astrologer* tell you is right for you? Then *just do it!*

TARGETING THE RIGHT GOALS

> **HOW WILL UNDERSTANDING YOUR CHART HELP YOU MAKE DECISIONS?**
>
> Knowing the basic rules of the new Money Astrology won't make you a professional astrologer, but at least you'll get a *feel* of the process for these four purposes:
>
> **(1) TO HELP YOU KNOW WHO YOU ARE BETTER:** you will get a better understanding of *who you are* through your chart, while strengthening your contact with your *inner astrologer*. While you are your own therapist.
>
> **(2) GUIDANCE DURING LIFE CRISES & TURNING POINTS:** I have discovered that most successful decision-makers normally do *not* need help interpreting their natal charts because they are already guided by their *inner astrologer* ... however, in a business or personal crisis occurs, it may be helpful to return to basics, review and recommit to your destiny, your mission and your life's goals.
>
> **(3) QUESTIONS FOR YOUR ASTROLOGER:** you should be better able to work with your astrologer without being confused by the buzzwords, and able to ask the right questions when you review your chart with any professional.
>
> **(4) THE BASIS FOR PREDICTING YOUR FUTURE:** and most importantly, you need an understanding of your *birth chart* as a basis for any future forecasts or predictions using your *upcoming cycles or transits* to make plan future business and financial decisions as discussed in Rules 2 & 3 below.
>
> Most books on astrology turn off readers because they are too esoteric and complicated. If the following method is still too complex, see my summary in Appendix Four, or call me. I'll help you get computer software for the job.

Let's keep it very simple. I'll tell you exactly what I do, my processes, my resources and what I look for in your chart. What I do may not be regarded as conventional by other professionals, but it works for me, and for my clients.

START WITH THE RIGHT ASTRONOMIC DATA BASE.

The basic facts are from astronomy and history. What's your birth data; the day and year you were born, the time of day, plus the location, that is, the city and state were you born in. That's all that the astrologer needs to calculate the positions of the planets from an *ephemeris,* a minute-to-minute calendar of planetary movements, calculated for NASA and other agencies.

Actually, I advise busy clients to work with a professional on this crucial beginner's stage, just as you'd hire an accountant or attorney for expert advice.

Of course, the simple solution is just to buy the astrological software, including the printed reports and then you've got them on your computer to work with and learn on. It's not very difficult and you'll probably enjoy it. Besides it's profitable for you.

You can save yourself a lot of time by investing in some of the excellent astrological software packages available for several hundred dollars, with the deluxe systems costing a thousand dollars or more. You might even start with some of the programs under fifty dollars that have interactive interpretations. I've tested one and found it helpful as an introduction.

Once installed, it actually takes longer to input a client's birth data than it does for the computer to calculate the positions of all the planets at the moment of your birth. In five minutes your astrologer, or you, will have a completed natal birth chart to work with. Several software publishers are listed in Appendix One as a resource if you decide to invest in a software system.

Now comes the tougher stuff, the analysis and interpretation. What in God's name do all those *astronomical* and *astrological* squiggles *mean?*

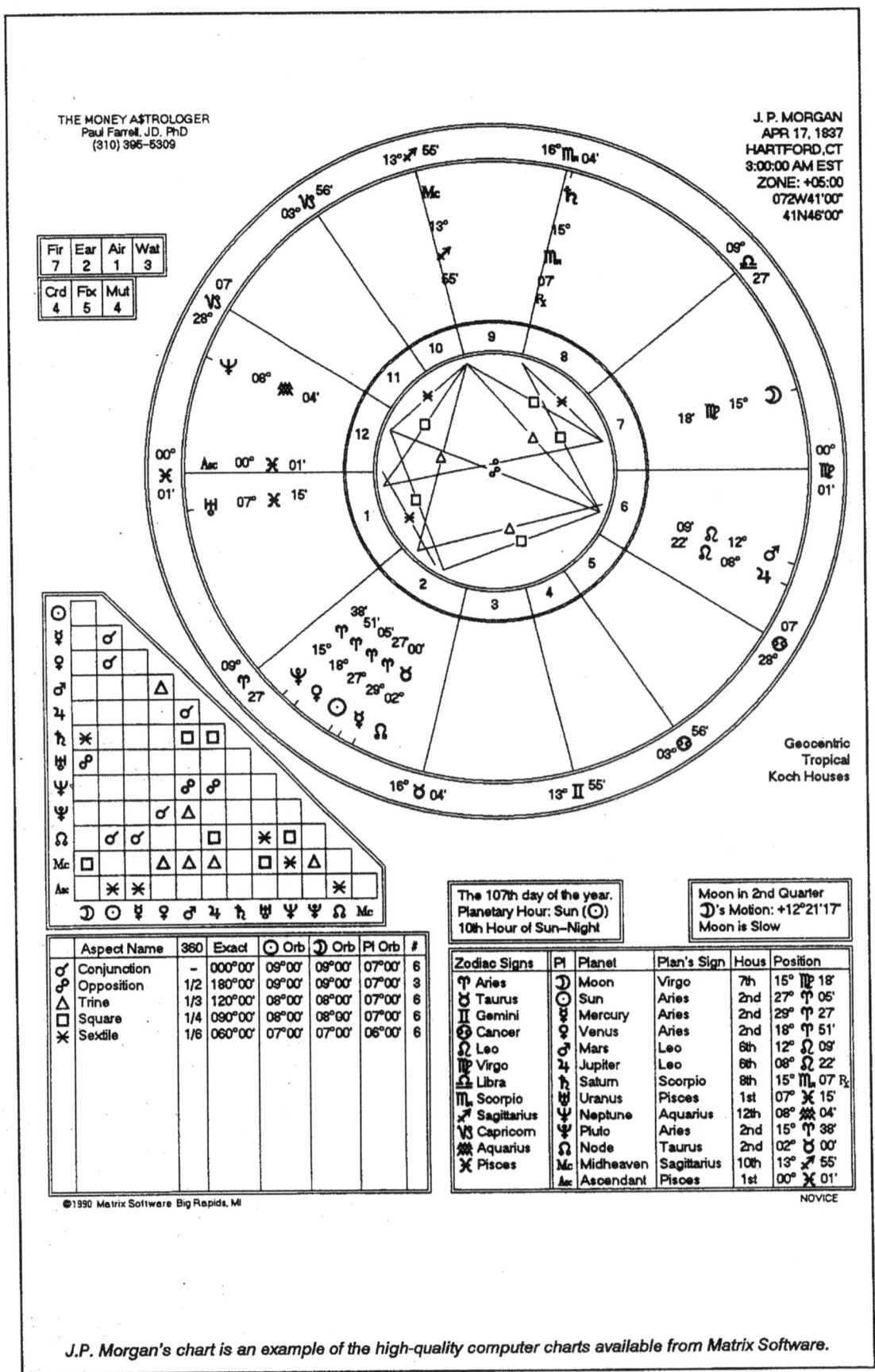

J.P. Morgan's chart is an example of the high-quality computer charts available from Matrix Software.

Targeting The Right Goals

YOUR ASTROLOGICAL INTERPRETATION:
THE SIX KEY POWER CENTERS MAKING *YOU* "OUT-STANDING"

Astrology is the interpretative side of astronomy, or as Henry Weingarten puts it, "astrology is a mathematical psychology based on astronomy."

This new Money Astrology is just a simple way of helping you identify your goals, by focusing you on the *6 key centers of power* that *stand out* of your birth chart. What's important, and what's not.

Start your analysis by asking: "What are the *outstanding power centers* located in your chart?" A workbook, like Bloch and Georges' *Astrology For Yourself*, or volume II of March & McEver's *The Only Way To Learn Astrology* might also help you structure your initial research and analysis.

If you focus on these *six outstanding* characteristics, these *stand-outs* will provide the basis for 95% of the interpretation of your goals. Although you may still need a professional to interpret your data, you should be familiar with this process so you can ask better questions and understand the results.

The "Quick'n'Dirty" Astro-Profile Analysis table in the Appendix Four summarizes this procedure if you are in a hurry. These *6 power centers* are:

POWER CENTER #ONE: THE HOUSE POSITIONS OF YOUR PLANETS.

In our 6,000 year history, the vast majority of traditional astrologers have placed their emphasis on the *Signs* of the planets ("What's your sign"). In the new astrology the *House* positions of the planets are key, building on the scientific research of Dr. Gauquelin. The 12 Houses are easily seen counting counter-clockwise from the Ascendant or Rising Sign on the horizon at the moment of your birth. Think of the houses as 12 rooms in a circular hotel tower, or 12 zones on a dartboard, each representing a part of your life.

You can review the interpretations of each of the planets based on *the houses* they are located in, with special emphasis on any planets that are in a *stellia* (a bunch of three or more planets) or *aspecting* (making certain angles) either the Midheaven or Ascendant.

> **AN EXAMPLE OF J. P. MORGAN, FINANCIER**
> Morgan's chart is a good example, with a heavy concentration of energies in even numbered houses; a total of 8 planets in the 2nd *(earnings)*, 6th *(work)*, 8th *(leveraged resources)*, and 12th ... suggesting a powerful man in business and finance, as well as a rational, left-brained human being. Another person with more planets in odd-numbered houses would be more right-brained and artistic.

This process is explained in more detail in Appendix Four; see the section, *Zip-Codes*, for your specific interpretations. Also, for this purpose, I recommend Volume I of the March and McEver series, *The Only Way To Learn Astrology*, which has some excellent interpretations focusing on business and careers.

The houses are your own personal photo of the sky as it was the moment you were born. There are 12 houses, just as there are 12 signs. Thus, two people born at precisely the same moment will have all their planets in exactly the same signs and relationships to each other, but since they're born in different locations, their house structures *will* be different, reflecting their uniqueness.

Consider, for example, twins born within minutes of each other in the same location. Even they will have slightly different charts, slightly different house set-ups and sometimes even different relationships between the planets. I recall one set of twins born just 5 minutes apart. They had only one slight difference on their charts; Jupiter, the planet of adventure, was in the second house (security-minded) for one, and the third house (child-like) for the other. Yet they were so different it was as if they had different parents, and they fit my interpretation to a tee.

> **SUCCESS TIP: HOUSES, NOT SIGNS ARE KEY TO THE NEW ASTROLOGY.** The shift in emphasis to the house positions of the planets from their signs may well be the *single most significant step* for the new astrology, mainly because it is scientifically grounded. However, most current astrologers will continue to emphasize the signs of the planets, out of habit, until the new generation of astrologers and the new paradigm of astrology is fully anchored.

In the emerging new astrology of the 21st century, the importance of the House positions of your planets will be understood as more important than their signs. In fact, Gauquelin's research studies showed *no statistical validity* to the signs, but did reinforce the importance of the house positions, especially for those planets located near the major axes.

POWER CENTER #TWO: PLANETS NEAR YOUR CHART'S MAIN AXES.

Specifically check your chart for any planets that are in the *Power Zones* identified by Michel Gauquelin. Basically that means the planets around your:

. **MIDHEAVEN, the North-South axis,** which reflects the relationship of your career and public life often as it conflicts with the family and home. Look especially for planets in 9th House and the first 10 degrees of the 10th House.

. **ASCENDANT, the East-West axis,** the horizon, your identity as reflected in your relationship to others. The Rising Sign is also called the Ascendant. Many astrologers today believe the Rising Sign along with the Moon are more important than the Sun sign. Look especially for planets in 12th House and the first 10 degrees of the 1st House.

You can also refer to Binder's *Planets In Work* for a mathematical description of Gauquelin's *Power Zones* (near the two main axes) and some excellent interpretations for each planet if located in one of these zones.

> **FOR EXAMPLE, MORGAN has one key planet in a *power zone*.** Saturn, a very important planet in defining business power is less than thirty degrees clockwise from his Midheaven axis. Saturn is the symbol of *authority*, and it is in his 8th house - *other people's money and resources* - banking and finance!

Next, review other planets *making aspects* to these power axes, that is, the Midheaven and the Ascendent. Look mainly for the Trines, Sextiles, Squares and Oppositions because they add power to your chart and to you. These aspects are defined below. For some very helpful interpretations, see Volume II of March and McEver's *The Only Way To Learn Astrology*.

POWER CENTER #THREE: YOUR PLANETS IN A SYNERGISTIC BUNCH.

Now look for any synergistic "bunches" of planets, *stellia* as the ancient astrologers call them. That is, you may have three or four planets located close

TARGETING THE RIGHT GOALS

together. When this happens they create a synergistic effect, with a higher concentration of electromagnetic energies focused like a laser beam. That gives added importance to the interpretation of their particular house and sign.

> **MORGAN IS A EXCELLENT EXAMPLE of this kind of concentration of focused energies** - with his four Aries planets in the 2nd house of earnings and values! Of course this man was born wealthy, however, his astrological chart also supports the fact that he would personally succeed in expanding his family's wealth and power, and do it in an Aries way, aggressive and entrepreneurial.

Pottenger's book has some interpretations of stellia in the last chapter. You can also use my Zip-Code table in Appendix Four, putting extra emphasis on the interpretation for the house and/or sign of the stellia.

POWER CENTER #FOUR: YOUR PLANETS IN THE 4 ELEMENTS.

The signs of the planets are still important as a secondary means of interpretation. Thus, while the sign of the Sun does not control your personality and career, the signs of *all 10 key planets become important as a* group, depending on which signs are *dominant*.

The signs group into one of the four *elements; fire, earth, air and water*. Each element has three signs with similar characteristics so you don't even need to focus on the specific signs. It's simple.

> **THE FOUR ASTROLOGICAL "ELEMENTS"**
> **FIRE POWER: Aries, Leo & Sagittarius** ... *Spirit, Intuition & Passion*
> **EARTH POWER: Taurus, Capricorn & Virgo** ... *Body, Assets & Sensations*
> **AIR POWER: Gemini, Libra & Aquarius** ... *Intellect & Communications*
> **WATER POWER: Cancer, Scorpio & Pisces** ... *Emotions & Consciousness*

There's nothing particularly new about classifying the world using these *four elements*. The term elements originated way before the early scientific classifications of what physicists and chemists now catalogue into more than 100 *elements,* everything from hydrogen and oxygen to uranium and plutonium.

The elements also have historical roots with the early religious leaders who have used this four-part division as a metaphysical way of viewing the world, reflected in the Bible. As the theologian Matthew Fox aptly said, "the psyche *is* the cosmos." Carl Jung also used the elements in his model of the human psyche, which in turn have been converted into some commonly used psychological tests of personality, such as the Meyers-Briggs Personality Types.

Look at the list of the "elements" on your computer printout. Which of the 4 elements is in high-profile, and what's missing? You should give extra weight to the signs of planets near the two primary axes, in Dr. Gauquelin *Power Zones,* noted in his book, *Written In The Stars,* and also in Jaime Binder's book, *Planets in Work.*

You should also check the table, *Ten Personality Profiles for Business Success,* in Appendix Four for various astro-psychological types, plus their potentials for success in various businesses and professions. Also look at any out-standing traditional interpretations using the signs. You should also see, Pottenger's book, *Complete Horoscope Interpretation,* and Arroyo's *Astrology, Psychology And The Four Elements.*

> FOR EXAMPLE, J. P. MORGAN is a very strong Fire personality, with six planets in Fire signs; four planets in Aries (Sun, Mercury, Venus and Pluto) and two in Aries (Mars and Jupiter). This man would make decisions on his gut instincts and collect information later. Definitely intuitive and passionate ... "Millionaires don't hire astrologers, billionaires do," he would blurt out publicly.
>
> If, however, Morgan had a Pisces Sun (a water sign), the combined power of his other planets in the fire signs would definitely override the Water Sun sign. In that case, focusing merely on the Sun sign would then be very misleading. Besides, the Moon sign is often more important than your Sun sign anyway, because it reflects your emotional energies, which often controls our reasoning. Morgan has a Virgo Moon (very critical and controlling emotionally) in the 7th House of partnerships and relationships, so he's likely to dominate everyone. If you want more on interpretations, see the Zip-Code Table in Appendix Four.

POWER CENTER #FIVE: STRUCTURES FORMED BY YOUR PLANETS.

Any two planets have a specific angular relationship between one and other. The *important* angles are called *aspects*, and are divided into either:

OPPORTUNITIES: mainly the Trines (120 degrees) and the Sextiles (60 degrees) create a very favorable mix of powers, but may also signal a tendency toward self-indulgence if the person is not self-motivated into action, or

CHALLENGES: the Squares (90 degrees) and Oppositions (180 degrees) which test the ability of two powers to merge successfully. They may also signal a tendency to self-sabotage, which if overcome, will then become a major source of personal power.

The Conjunctions (zero degrees) may be either opportunities or challenges, depending on which two planets we're looking at, but more on them later. Any of these aspects may interact with and reinforce other energies in a person's chart, magnifying the power of other opportunities and challenges.

> SUCCESS TIP: Remember, none of these aspects are inherently *good* or *bad*. My recommendation is that you look at every aspect as *both* an opportunity *and* a challenge, mere lessons for this life-time. It all depends on how you "play the game." Indeed, I find that it is often in how we respond to life's challenges that we truly discover who we are, and also uncover our greatest rewards. For as Nietzsche once said, "that which does not destroy us will set us free."

Also look for other special configurations. Sometimes several aspects combine to create even larger configurations, the main ones are:

. GRAND TRINES AS OPPORTUNITIES: (3 planets 120 degrees apart) usually represent an opportunity, for example, a Grand Water Trine suggests a highly creative individual, while a Fire Trine suggests a very dramatic promoter, and an entrepreneurial personality needing center stage, and

. T-SQUARES AS CHALLENGES: (3 planets, with 2 of them in opposition to each other 180 degrees apart and both squaring the 3rd planet), which are generally considered a major challenge for you, one that can hold you back *or make you stronger*.

TARGETING THE RIGHT GOALS 55

> **THE MORGAN EXAMPLE:** His chart has a example of a very powerful Grand Trine in the Fire signs, further empowering his fiery personality. His Midheaven (career and public standing) Trines Jupiter and Mars in the 6th House, as well as Venus, a money planet, in the 2nd House of earnings. More importantly, this shows that his career, work and earnings are all in a close working balance.
>
> Morgan also has a T-Square - an opposition between Neptune in the 12th House and the Jupiter-Mars conjunction (adventurer and entrepreneur) in the Sixth House (very big dreams), with Saturn squaring them (can't see his weak own points). He was a world conqueror, and his chart reflected his powers.

Each of these structures adds a special kind of power to a chart, depending on the planets involved. See Volume II of March and McEver. Also, in *Astrology, Karma & Transformation,* Arroyo notes, "Rather than focusing upon the type of configuration ... one must understand primarily the meaning of the planets involved and their specific interchanges with the other planets in the configuration ... they all represent particularly intensified interactions of the energies ..." You can use the Zip-Codes for an initial interpretation of the planets, making sure you also give full consideration to the houses they are located in, as well as their signs.

POWER CENTER #SIX: YOUR PLANETS MAKING A UNIQUE PATTERN.

Next, take look at the overall appearance of your chart. Are all the planets in half the chart, called a "bowl," suggesting an imbalance or one-sidedness, and that something's missing. Also, does one planet gain extra power, because it is separated from the rest of the pattern, creating a "bucket" or "fan" formation? And so on. Jaime Binder's *Planets In Work* for great interpretations of the main patterns. Volume II of the March and McEver's series is also excellent.

YOU DON'T HAVE TO BE AN EXPERT TO "KNOW YOURSELF!"

Once you get the hang of it, you can get a reasonable good fix on anybody in less than half an hour, even if you don't have an astrologer around to do the analysis for you. You'll also be better prepared to ask your astrologer the right questions and understand the answers.

A half hour is certainly less time than it would take to analyze and make a decision on investing in a new project, corporate bond or real estate deal. Of course you'll probably want a *second opinion* if you are analyzing it yourself. But this process will give you a big clue as to the process your astrological consultant is using, and the kind of questions you might ask them in getting a *second opinion.*

Better yet, my advice is that you start by buying some astrological software, printing a report on the subject in question, then reading the report thoroughly. Think of it like doing your *due diligence* or running a Dun and Bradstreet credit check. The only danger is that, like a lot of financial documents and computer-generated accounting reports, these astrological profiles have a lot of information, usually too much, and it takes an expert astrologer to pick the wheat from the chaff.

THE QUANTUM LEAP: RE-DISCOVERING YOUR DESTINY!

Now you have to integrate all this data, and in the end you will discover that astrology is as much an art as a science, and from that perspective the work of an astrological counselor is not unlike the work of other professionals; lawyers, accountants, physicians, psychologists, advertising executives and management consultants.

Just as business consulting and psychological counseling are both interactive processes, so is the work between the client and the astrologer acting as a dynamic team. Personally, I never just sit and pontificate. And as a client, your key guideline throughout should be, "Does it *feel* right, that is, are your guts in sync with what your astrologer's conclusions?" Trust that intuition. If it does feel right, it's probably coming from your center, your *inner astrologer*.

MONEY DECISIONS: THE FINAL LEAP OF FAITH
The information you and your astrologer generate during the above six steps should take you 90% of the way through your analysis. After that, you'll have to make an intuitive leap of faith to get you the rest of the way, and only trial-and-error experience will help you succeed over the long haul. When I was at Morgan Stanley I had to do it often, spending months collecting data then having to make a final leap, *a guess-timate* that didn't always seem to jibe with the facts, but still felt right in my gut.

Any business executive, accountant, lawyer or other professional will understand *leaping* ... after all the meetings, data collecting, forecasting and strategizing, you're *forced* to make a decision. It's that last 10% of the way that is *beyond all the rational numbers-crunching, it is a creative leap of faith into the unknown, based solely on a feeling in your guts, and a vision.*

If it is *right* - that is, *in harmony with your destiny* - it will intuitively "feel" right and you'll flow with it easily and naturally. That happened to me in 1975 when I wrote a 40 page screenplay treatment in less than a month after my first astrologer said I should have been in film, television or musical comedy, not having ever thought of such writing. My first astrologer's comments obviously *felt* so "right" to me that I went quickly and passionately into this exciting new adventure of the hero.

THE JOURNEY OF THE HERO ... THE POWER OF A DREAM

The purpose of this first rule in the new Money Astrology process of decision-making is to help you *focus on the right target*, on *your* mission and *your* goals. It is a process of discovering who you are, of learning to *know thyself*, as Plato once said. Once you understand the inner you ... your destiny, your vision, your mission, your goals will naturally unfold, *they will demand action!*

No wonder so many feel like they are playing in the wrong "game of life," or playing the game in the wrong stadium. We have become a nation of career nomads. Like *E.T.* and *Starman*, searching for a way back home, or like Luke Skywalker, obsessed with becoming a Jedimaster, or Richard Dreyfuss in *Close Encounters*, obsessive, driven to discover some elusive "mission" in life.

Joseph Campbell calls this vision quest "The Journey of The Hero," urging us to "follow our bliss." Down *The Road Less Travelled*, Dr. Scott Peck might add.

Carl Jung called this inner compulsion, "The Way of Individuation." It is within each of us driving us to fulfill our destiny. It is a lifelong process raising us *from* the powerlessness of childhood dependencies *to* the empowerment of mature self-realization. On a more practical level, the author and psychologist Marsha Sinetar tells us to *Do What You Love And The Money Will Follow*.

Yet all too often The Path is obscured and fogbound. You start out knowing where you're headed (or think you know), but go *off-course*. You may at times believe that you have *arrived* at your destination, only to discover that it has been moved. Or, you may see your target clearly, but you've lost the drive, the

Targeting The Right Goals 57

passion. Your energy has disappeared, and you abandon the journey. The scenarios are endless. The bottom-line is a temporary absence of your sense of mission.

A vision quest - the passionate pursuit of your mission - often requires a total reexamination of your astrological DNA, the destiny imprinted by the universe on your genes. Your mission *is* reflected in your birth chart. You can discover it now, beginning with the excellent career planning guides currently available, resources that build on Dr. Gauquelin's scientific research.

Discover your target, and pursue it with passion!

SUCCESS GOALS: A NEW CAREER ... EVERY 10 YEARS!
Does your career path reflect current research results: that 83% of all college graduates no longer work in their major field of study by age 40; that the 3% of Yale alumni who graduated with *specific* goals were making more money than the other 97% of their classmates 20 years later; and that today's graduates will make at least 3 *major* career changes in their life-time.

Maybe you can do without goals. Rush Limbaugh, that inimical "role model for entrepreneurs," said in *Success* magazine, "Goals are too limiting. I just knew I wanted *more.*" Yet Napoleon Hill sees it differently, "the Creator seems to favor those who *know precisely what they want and what they do not want.*" Astrology may just be the "edge" you need to help you make more profitable decisions!

HOW YOU CAN ESCAPE A "MID-LIFE CRISIS" & OTHER TURNING POINTS

You may have heard of or even experienced the so-called mid-life crisis. Some time ago I focused my doctoral dissertation on this life-cycle, interviewing men. I saw a definite increase in the number of career changes, marriage break-ups, geographic relocations and addictive behaviors. Freud, Jung and many other psychologists have identified this and many other predictable phases in our lives. One especially good book on the subject is Mayer's *Male Mid-Life Crisis*.

When I began my work in astrology I was fascinated to discover that many of our *psychological* life-cycles could be predicted by looking for certain astrological transits.

For example, the mid-life transition is tied to the timing of three transits in your chart; Pluto-square-Pluto, Uranus-opposite-Uranus and Neptune-square-Neptune, all of which will happen once in your life, around age forty. While you are in the energies of these transits (for about two years), they'll dominate your business and personal life, over-powering other transits.

As a result, a large number of clients seek advice during this mid-life crisis period, *because it's tough to escape from these energies*. Still, it's better to know the facts in advance - and work with it to your advantage - rather than think you're going crazy.

You may not be able to totally escape the crisis, but you certainly can discover in it the "seed of an equivalent benefit," as Napoleon Hill would say.

The Astrology Of Successful Decision-Making

2. THE RIGHT TIMING FOR <u>YOUR</u> DECISIONS
TURNING POINTS, TRANSITIONS & ACTIONS

SUCCESS RULE #2.
KNOW YOUR POWER DAYS, THE CHALLENGES & OPPORTUNITIES, LEARN TO PREDICT THE BEST TIME FOR YOUR DECISIONS. THEN PLAN AHEAD & GO FOR IT!

If you're genuinely interested in using astrology to help you make business, financial, investment and career planning decisions, one book is a *must-read* ... *Cycles, The Mysterious Forces That Trigger Events,* the classic published in 1971 by Edward Dewey, founder and first President of the Foundation for the Study of Cycles, with the help of co-author Og Mandino, editor of *Success* magazine.

THE KEY TO PREDICTING BUSINESS & FINANCIAL FUTURES ... CYCLES

Cycles is *not* a book about astrology, and yet, indirectly, it is probably the best introduction to astrology. In fact, the Foundation and its scientific researchers tactfully avoid all astrological *interpretations*. Instead, they focus on the scientific process, statistically *observing* and recording the existence of natural & business cycles. What they observe is worth your closest attention.

CYCLES: THE MYSTERIOUS FORCES THAT TRIGGER EVENTS
"The science of cycles deals with events that reoccur with reasonable regularity. Such events may be in nature, business, or anything else. The important thing about regularity is that it implies predictability. And if you know that an event is coming, you can often prevent it or avoid it if you wish. Or if you cannot prevent it or avoid it, you can at least prepare for it so that its effect on your life is lessened.

"Most people do not realize the extent to which cycles and regularities exist in the world. Here are a few examples:" And the authors then begin a long list that includes:

. wheat production, heart disease, salmon fishing, and the abundance of rabbits, lynx, owls and hawks all follow on a 9.6 year cycle,

. grasshoppers, however, appear in excess in 9.2 year cycles, and plagues of mice is 4 year cycles, during presidential election years,

. church memberships, sunspot eruptions, fashion trends, lake levels, glaciers melting, earthquakes, tornadoes and other weather patterns, pine cone production, cancer reoccurrences and other diverse natural events occur regular cycles,

. real estate activities, commodity prices, industrial accidents and men's emotions, business sales, cheese consumption, marriages and births, the effectiveness of advertising, wars and even political landslides follow cyclical patterns, thus lending some predictability to the process.

"Many cycles in nature seem to have the same wavelength as cycles in human affairs, and some cycles found on earth seem to have the same wavelength as cycles found on the sun. The other planets may even be involved, and the implications are strong that the solution to the mystery of the cause of cycles will be discovered somewhere in the universe - *somewhere out there.*"

More important for us, Dewey notes that there is "a synchronicity of turning points ... *substantially all the cycles of any given length turn at about the same time.*" In other words, I can predict future events, in nature, in business cycles, in the stock market, and in human behavior, both mine and yours.

Here in Rule Two we'll focus on *your* turning points. Later, in Rule Three, the astrology of "Predicting Your Competition's Future Decisions," we'll focus on forecasting "*their*" future, that is, other people and the public as a whole. And we'll set-up some guidelines for your responses.

WHY IS THE OLD FARMERS ALMANAC 80% ACCURATE?

Since ancient times, farmers have asked, "When will it rain?" Indeed, the role of early astrologers was tied to weather predicting: the effects of moon phases, sun spots and other astro-cycles on rainfall, planting and harvesting.

> **LONG-RANGE WEATHER PREDICTIONS ... FROM PLANETARY CYCLES**
> "In its two hundred years of publication, the Old Farmer's Almanac has distinguished itself with year-in-advance whether predictions. Informal surveys in various regional newspapers and other periodicals have often credited the Almanac with 80 percent accuracy, a better track record than the high-powered government-financed weather bureau," says Vivian Martin, a journalist, in her eminently readable, *Astro-cycles.*
> "What is the secret of the Almanac makers' success? They're discreet up in Dublin, New Hampshire, but editor Susan Peery reveals that 'natural cycles' are at the heart of the 'secret formula' that almanac founder Robert B. Thomas developed and passed down to Almanac meteorologists ... astronomic phenomena are the main determinants of our weather."

Let's face it, we already know about the Moon's effects on us. You can actually *watch* the Moon's daily power over the tides. And on a Full Moon you *feel* its influence everywhere. If our bodies are made up of 85% water, you *know* the Moon has enormous influence over you, affecting everything, your body, your mind, and your emotions.

If you think you get whacked out by a cycle of the Full Moon ... *what about the cycles of the other planets?*

They all influence you! Each has enormous powers, influencing you in its own unique way. We are creatures of habit, influenced by many planetary cycles, including daily circadian cycles of the spinning earth, monthly lunar cycles, and our seasonal trips around the sun. *Every day the power of the planets influence everyone on Earth, and no one can escape their powers.*

CYCLES & TURNING POINTS: YOUR KEY TO PRACTICAL DECISIONS

Success in business is often tied to our ability to predict, forecast and anticipate major turning points ... *and the best timing for a decision.*

When all is going smoothly, we tend to settle into routines or stable habit patterns. We have less incentive or motivation for change and transform. We relax our guard, and become vulnerable in our conviction that all will continue to progress favorably ahead.

In the back of our minds we may occasionally reflect on the old adage, *what goes up must come down,* but we usually ignore this reality while we enjoy the current ride, scooping up our goodies. The same is true for the problem areas. They never last, eventually everything changes and they fade, too.

THE RIGHT TIME FOR YOUR DECISIONS

An important key to success is knowing how to predict, forecast, estimate, anticipate, foreshadow, expect, calculate or plan and budget for major turning points ... the cycles both up and down!

The key turning points in your life could include;
- **strategic changes in a business venture,**
- **highs and lows in the securities markets,**
- **real estate investment decisions,**
- **opportunities and losses in partnerships,**
- **challenges to your physical health,**
- **developmental and situational life crises.**

If you are able to anticipate change, you have the opportunity to consciously control life's turning points by your decisions. Then you have better control of your destiny because now you can work *with* the coming change, transform and renew who you are. You become a part of the paradigm shift, rather than an obstacle to it.

Each of us is on our special *Journey of The Hero*, with many twists and turns along the path. Astrologers, the original *psychologists of antiquity* according to Jung, have long been aware of these life cycles, transitions and other turning points, such as the midlife crisis. At these turning points, we are force us to confront and transform ourselves, and the world around us.

NEW SOFTWARE: NOW YOU CAN PRINT YOUR OWN DAILY HOROSCOPE.

In order to effectively make a decision, you must first be able to identify and predict these turning points. That's where your transits or astrological cycles come in. They are the keys to assisting you at these career, business and financial junctures. In short, you really must know how to work with these transits in order to succeed. Start with a forecast of your transits.

In order to give you a solid overview of your life, both in the recent past and near future, a review of your transits should cover the past few months and at least a full year ahead, with a detailed look at the next business quarter. See the one-page example included at the end of this chapter.

A TRANSIT FORECAST: CREATING YOUR DAILY BUSINESS HOROSCOPE.
The first thing you will need is a print-out of your *hit list*, which is just a day-by-day schedule of your *transits*, the *dynamic* angular relationships between:

1. YOUR NATAL PLANETS AT THE MOMENT OF BIRTH, your genetic fingerprints, your cosmic DNA, in other words, your "chart." By definition, these positions of your natal planets never change during your lifetime, they are fixed at the moment of your birth; and

2. THE CURRENT POSITIONS OF THE PLANETS as they move in their unique cycles through the universe, making *different* angles to *each* person's chart.

You can get a forecast of your transits printed with or without interpretations. In the early stages, I strongly recommend that you save your time and begin by using someone else's interpretations. The computer services companies will sell you individual reports or the necessary computer software.

All this information about the location of the planets at *any second - past, present or future* - has been calculated for the federal government agencies, N.A.S.A. and Jet Propulsion Laboratories, and is currently available on relatively inexpensive computer software. The Matrix Software's BlueStar program is quite excellent, as is Astrolabe's NOVA software.

Your hit list of transits can become quite long if you include *all* the fast moving planets. So, until you become familiar with the level of information you need for your particular style of decision-making, I suggest you:
. either print-out just one month, or at the most, three months at a time,
. or, limit your hit list to the transits of the *outer* planets, which move through the zodiac in relatively slow cycles (the time in each of the 12 houses varies depending on your birth chart, and it is not the same for every person):

TIMING OF THE OUTER PLANETS AROUND THE SUN & IN THE HOUSES

JUPITER	12 years (1 year in each house)	
	expansion, ideals, philosophy, travel, optimism, success	
SATURN	29 years (2.4 years)	
	contraction, discipline, limits, results, structure, reality	
URANUS	84 years (7 years)	
	individualism, originality, independence, freedom,	
NEPTUNE	165 years (14 years)	
	spirituality, creativity, fantasy, dreams, music, unity	
PLUTO	248 years (20.7 years)	
	transformation, power, rebirth, intensity, passion	

In addition, these outer planets have a greater transformational impact on your behavior and life, so they deserve more attention.

You may also want to print out your transits of the faster-moving planets, Mars (22 months), Venus (7.5 months) and Mercury (88 days). While these transits are important in *financial astrology* predicting *their* behavior, discussed in Rule 3, in *personal astrology* these faster moving transits do *not* have the same transformational impact on you as the outer planets' transits.

Remember, transits of the faster-moving planets occur quite frequently, like ripples on a vast ocean. If you do print out these faster moving transits, limit them to the next month. Otherwise, you will bury the important data in a very long and confusing printout of less important information. Enough to make you run away from astrology forever.

If you want to stay focused on the bigger picture, if you are centered on your mission, if you are coming from an awareness of the synchronistic bond between your genes and the universal cycles, you will be careful about giving your personal decision-making power to some expert on Moon wobbles, Mercury retrogrades, or whatever, even if they're successfully using this information to make stock market trades and they have a trackrecord to prove it!

STEP #1: STRATEGIC CYCLES ... YOUR *HOUSE* TRANSITS

In order to understand the longer-range context, look for the current house transits of Jupiter (a force of growth and expansion) and Saturn (structure and limitation) in your chart. The transits of these two planets are the best guidelines of your current *psychological* life-cycle, the setting for your *business decisions.*

RESOURCE TOOLS: For your interpretations of the transits, here are some of the better guidebooks to help you in this process, written by a few excellent psychologically-trained astrologers. In particular see:
. Hand, *Planets in Transit* (considered the Bible of the industry)
. Arroyo, *Astrology, Karma & Transformation; Relationships & Life Cycles*
. Townley, *Astrological Life Cycles ... Personal & Career Opportunities*

THE RIGHT TIME FOR YOUR DECISIONS

Jupiter & Saturn: "Practical Tools" For Understanding Your Life-Cycles.
Stephen Arroyo, an astrologer and psychotherapist, is rather emphatic about the need to focus primarily on the outer planets, "you could throw out all the rest of astrology and just using Jupiter and Saturn ... transiting your natal houses, you would have such a practical tool that it would be better than any other method (in dealing with the cyclical) nature of important developments, changes and growth periods in your life."

Arroyo's advice has proven quite accurate in my work, so let's see how to apply it, as an example of transit analysis and interpretation. If you set it up properly, your *Transit Forecast Report* will identify which houses Jupiter and Saturn are currently transiting in your natal chart. Note that their energies represent totally opposite life-cycle influences:

HOUSE TRANSITS of JUPITER & SATURN: A STUDY IN CONTRASTS

Jupiter Expands You: Jupiter takes 12 years to transit your natal chart, often acting like *an angel on your shoulder,* guiding you. Jupiter's transformational power influences each house for about a year, encouraging your growth in your career and personal life. Jupiter's power is *expansive.* Jupiter inspires a more comprehensive, optimistic approach. During Jupiter transits you may be inspired to *enlarge* yourself in the house it's transiting.

Saturn Restricts You: as it transits your natal chart over 29 years. Saturn creates opportunities to build stronger foundations during the 2.4 years it takes to move through each house. Saturn's power *restricts.* Saturn forces us into a deeper, more practical and disciplined restructuring of our consciousness. During Saturn transits you often discover and obtain what is really important in your life, not always what you want, but what you need. In the process, however, you are often painfully forced to *let go of old ideas* and old relationships that are no longer productive, *before you can move on.*

THE HOUSE TRANSITS: JUPITER EXPANDS & SATURN CONTRACTS HERE

HOUSES	YOUR AREAS OF GROWTH & CHANGE
1st house	**THE POWER START** initiative, commitment, action, doing own thing
2nd house	**STAYING POWER** earning power, basic values, finances, resources
3rd house	**BRAIN POWER** mental reasoning, ideas, learning, communication
4th house	**INNER POWER** family, home, foundations, roots, past history
5th house	**POWER CENTRAL** self-expression, creativity, speculation, love
6th house	**THE POWER MACHINE** service to others, health, work, research
7th house	**A BALANCE OF POWER** business relations, marriage, compete, cooperate
8th house	**THE POWER BROKER** leverage in emotions, sexuality, money & spirit
9th house	**THE POWER ELITE** higher mind, truth-seeking, travel, self-discovery
10th house	**PEAK POWER** career, reputation, public power & recognition
11th house	**POWERS OF MIND** goals, groups, social network, uniqueness in world
12th house	**YOUR HIGHER POWER** behind scenes, secrets, subconscious, spirituality

Check your print-out report and look for growth opportunities in each of the houses being transited by Jupiter and Saturn. Consider the general descriptions of the life areas influenced by each house on the above table, while keeping in mind the opposing natures of the two planets, Jupiter expanding and Saturn contracting. Here are a couple examples:

> **EXAMPLE #1 - SATURN:** if the transiting Saturn is in your 5th natal house, you might feel restricted in the way you express yourself, you might feel "parental" in your love relationships and that children are a burden, you might also lean toward buying bonds rather than stocks in the marketplace, and your creative spark may not be as spontaneous as it has been at other times in your life. However, you may well be more focused and structured in the things that you create and the methods you use to create them, and you could also have the urge to study some new technology.

> **EXAMPLE #2 - JUPITER:** My experience confirms the wisdom of Arroyo's advice. This book was written when Jupiter was transiting my 1st House, starting a new phase in my life, *and my soul poured into the book*. Moreover, during the month Jupiter was also trining Mercury, the planet of mental thinking and communications. Five years earlier, when Jupiter transited into my 9th house (a Gauquelin Power Zones) I closed down a successful business and traveled to the Esalen Institute, a New Age community, as a work-scholar for a few months. And when Saturn was in my 12th house, another Gauquelin Power Sector, I virtually went into hibernation, separating from the real world, while hooking up with the collective unconscious.

Generally, your house transits of Saturn and Jupiter will give you a fairly good interpretation of your longer-range life-cycle.

STEP #2: YOUR DECISIONS TODAY ... THE PLANET-TO-PLANET TRANSITS!

In addition to the house transits, which usually influence you for a year or longer, your transit report will also have a second major set of transits, the daily planet-to-planet transits. Two technical points are important in order for you to understand the power of these daily transits:

First: The Energy Of The Transit Will Build Gradually. Your Transit Forecast will show you where the transits peak. However, their electromagnetic energies will be building, like slow-motion ocean waves, sometimes for weeks or months in advance, and diminishing for a period afterwards, with the build-up and decline forming a bell-shaped curve. Thus, you may well have *overlapping energy waves* influencing you simultaneously. Moreover, they may even be conflicting energies, but we already know life can sometimes be a mass of contradictions, dilemmas, paradoxes and double binds.

Second: Retrogrades Spread Out The Transit's Energies. The outer planets usually "retrograde" during most transit cycles, so you will get three hits of the same energy, usually spread out over a six-to-twelve month period. Of course the planets are not actually going backward, it just appears that way from our perspective on Earth, because of the differing speeds of the planets around the Sun. With these retrogrades, the electromagnetic *power* of the transit *peaks* three times, giving us three opportunities to hear its *message* and learn the *lesson* it carries. In between, the energy slacks off a bit.

Of course you are most likely going to rely on a computer-generated transit report, but I still believe that even the novice can interpret the transits using their hit list and their gut intuition, blending the individual powers of the two planets in

THE RIGHT TIME FOR YOUR DECISIONS

question (using the Zip-Code as a guide for each planet), and keeping in mind the following general meanings for the kind of transit printed on your forecast.

> **POWER DAYS: A SIMPLE METHOD OF "SCORING" YOUR TRANSITS**
>
> **1. OPPORTUNITIES**: the Trines (120 degrees) and Sextiles (60 degrees) create a *favorable* blending of the energies the two planets represent as we saw in the last chapter,
>
> **2. CHALLENGES**: the Squares (90 degrees) and Oppositions (180 degrees) which *test* your ability to successfully *blend or merge* the potentially *conflicting* energies of the two planets in the transit, and
>
> **3. CONJUNCTIONS**: technically, the Conjunctions (zero degrees) can be either opportunities or challenges, depending on the specific energies of the two planets. At this stage, just ask your *inner astrologer* if you have no other interpretation available, or if you don't quite feel right with the printed blurb. *Then trust your inner astrologer.*
> Here's another rule: you could also treat *all* conjunctions as opportunities if you're basically an *optimist*, and as challenges if you're a *realist*.

Finally, transits are constantly overlapping and interacting with each other, reinforcing or even cancelling their energies, especially when you have more than one key transit falling on a particular day. Major turning points are likely to occur for you when several transits all hit you about the same time, intensifying their total energies, or when there are no transits and you have no guideline.

A MORNING REVIEW of YOUR DAILY TRANSIT FORECAST

Now, armed with this perspective about the transits and a forecast of your transits, you can now review all your interpretations the house *and* the planet-to-planet transits. You will be reviewing the meaning of *all the transiting planets* as they impact all the planets on *your natal chart,* including the faster ones, the Moon, Sun, Mercury, Venus and Mars.

For example, in any one day you'll probably have an average of two or three transits to interpret, so it should be no big deal for you. *Many of my clients treat their transit reports like the front page of the Wall Street Journal, or one of those helpful one-day-at-a-time motivational books ... its another "information source" to be reviewed early in the business day, or when planning future actions.*

> **HOW ONE INTERNATIONAL BUSINESSMAN USES HIS TRANSIT FORECAST**
>
> **Here's an example of something you might try as a starter. One of my clients gets his transits updated regularly. He's an entrepreneur, an importer-exporter of heavy equipment. His transits are right next to his telephone, reviewed daily. Recently he told me that he ripped out the pages covering the ten days of his trip to Taiwan and put them right next to his telephone in the hotel.**
>
> **This man is very rational and a very successful entrepreneur. He claims that he always finds something to guide him, no matter what his horoscope report's advice may be, *favorable or not*.**
>
> **Although he's American-born, he instinctively uses astrology like the I Ching or the Tarot, or like von Oech's Whack Pack, as a technique of self-discovery, or a way of meditating to uncover what his *still small voice*, the *inner astrologer* is telling him is an appropriate action for the day. And why not, it is synchronistically tied to the transits, those electromagnetic energies of the planets.**

> **THE THREE MOST COMMON PATTERNS WITH YOUR FUTURE TRANSITS**
>
> With some experience, you'll notice the basic patterns describing the flow of all planet-to-planet transits over any given six-to-twelve month period. On the average you will only experience two or three transits of the outer planets in a given month, and these typically flow in one of the following three patterns:
>
> **JET TAKE-OFF.** Frequently I'll see a chart with very few challenging transits, and loaded with opportunities. In fact, the flow looks too good to be true. Actually I'll usually see someone with this pattern coming up in the near future, whereas they have just completed a very trying set of transits. They're talking to me because they instinctively know they've turned a corner, but they want some confirmation that their *trial by fire is* passing. *They're ready to take-off!*
>
> While this pattern may indicate a period of personal growth and career success, high expectations may also lead to self-indulgence and a failure to take full advantage of this favorable environment. It is vitally important to get into action and capitalize on these opportunities in your business and personal lives.
>
> **WHITE WATER RAFTING.** This overall pattern fits perhaps forty percent of the clients, some opportunities for growth and some challenges that prevent complacency, to keep them on their toes and in action. This pattern is a "white water rafting trip down the Grand Canyon" because of its choppy ups-and-downs. With this pattern it is important to look closely at the timing of the individual transits, and how they interact as you go from the peaks to the valleys.
>
> **BURN-OUT.** These clients may avoid astrologers because I rarely see people in this kind of cycle. Here most of the individual transits are on a down-trend, with a lot of challenges. One client had six of seven key transits in challenging and even health-threatening positions, all within two months *after* visiting me. Six days after I saw her, she went into a hospital for a month, which was no surprise to me.

SUMMARY: USING TRANSITS FOR DECISION-MAKING - 3 SIMPLE STEPS.

Use astrology as you would any other resource intended to sharpen your skills in making profitable decisions, remembering that ultimately you still must make the decision. If you want to start using the new astrology in your decision-making, begin with these three simple steps and ease into the process:

FIRST: PURCHASE A BASIC BOOK ON TRANSITS.
My advice is to get *one* book interpreting transits and become familiar with it by using it with your astrological hit list on a regular basis. Robert Hand's book, *Planets In Transits,* is the Bible of the astrological industry. Although there are others with shorter descriptions, if you want a quickie reference. Hand gets into the deeper psychological meaning of the transits, which is very helpful.

SECOND: BUY SOME ASTROLOGICAL COMPUTER SOFTWARE.
In addition to a resource book, each of the main software suppliers - Matrix, AIR, Astrolabe, and others - have computer software that makes this whole process *very easy*. That is, with this software you can *print* your own personal horoscope every day, based on your transits instead of the meaningless stuff in your newspaper. These suppliers will sell you reporting systems that do all this interpretation for you along with their calculation systems.

These reports will even tell you when their energy build-up begins and ends. They are written by some of the best minds in the field of astrology. For less than a thousand dollars you can own this software and print your own daily transits forever, for you and everyone else you need a fix on. Call and get their

THE RIGHT TIME FOR YOUR DECISIONS

catalogs, and check with me about our Money A$trology version of the transit forecasts, *Power Days*.

THIRD: WORK WITH AN EXPERIENCED ASTROLOGER, AS A MENTOR.

In order to master anything - aikido, commodities trading, sky diving, or astrology - you can accelerate the process and avoid many of the pitfalls by working with a skilled trainer for a period of time, at least until you master the fundamentals. Select someone who respects your *inner astrologer*, and then use them as a professional sounding-board for the bigger decisions.

One final word of caution. If you do buy the computer software and print out all the transits, including those of faster planets (the Moon, Mercury, Venus and Mars) be aware that their transits will greatly outnumber the transits of the slower planets. So please be careful. *Do not to give equal weight to all these transits, experience will help you here.*

In addition, you will quickly discover that these transit reports usually have no more than three or four lines of information interpreting each transit, so if you want more depth, I recommend you keep a copy of Robert Hand's *Planets In Transit* right there next to your printed report, and refer to it when you are making key decisions.

BOTTOM-LINE: THE TRANSITS WILL FORECAST YOUR "POWER DAYS!"

Know your cycles and transits well, they define your *Power Days*.

Your personal power will be substantially increased by understanding the cycles of your life. These business and life-cycles will become apparent to you in studying your current planetary transits.

Directly confront the demands of your current life-cycle transition and *work with* its lessons and opportunities. By taking active responsibility you are guaranteed new power and peace of mind.

If you can anticipate and predict the turning points in your life, big or small, you will be better able to use them to your advantage, whether they are opportunities or challenges, good fortunes or losses, gifts or failings.

The art and science of astrology is developing as a means of forecasting these turning points, helping you make the right decisions and leading you into the right actions. Having a roadmap in advance allows you to plan your alternatives ahead of time, marshall your resources, raise your spirits, and then get into action and go for the gold!

In the final analysis every transit and life-cycle is just a learning experience. You can learn anything you chose, positive or negative.

SUCCESS TIP: "Mastery is not perfection. But rather a journey, and the true master must be willing to try and fail and try again," says George Leonard, aikido trainer and author of *Mastery* and several other books on peak performance. Sound advice for anyone predicting the future, regardless of the method used.

YOUR "POWER DAYS" ... a Sample Transit Forecast

OCT 20 CHALLENGE: JU-SQR-PL (OCT 15-26)
You are in power-drive, wanting to **achieve something.** However, if it's blind faith and an obsession, you'll just stir up **opposition and conflict. Authorities in the commercial world** are likely to rebel against your drive to succeed. Temper ambition with tact. **Lead,** but be sensitive to others.

OCT 21 OPPORTUNITY: VE-TRI-ME (OCT 20-22)
Today you have a special gift with words and ideas, take advantage of it. Look for opportunities to **communicate, in trainings, sales and marketing, story-telling, brain-storming, negotiating,** advising and counseling. You **sell** yourself and your ideas with creativity, drama and **hi-tech technology.**

OCT 22 OPPORTUNITY: SU 2nd HOUSE (OCT 22 - NOV 21)
During the next month you are likely to be **building a strong foundation** for **new projects** developed recently. Now is a good time to do some **strategic planning, budget resources and get your plan into action.** Just be careful, avoid becoming too possessive or materialistic.

OCT 24 CHALLENGE: SU-SQR-VE (OCT 23-25)
Today your sense of values may be out-of-whack. **Be cautious** about any decisions involving **assets, investments, properties,** even design choices such as colors. Your decisions may be too flamboyant when you review them on a more conservative day. **Get third-party opinions.**

OCT 25 CHALLENGE: SU-OPP-UR (OCT 24-26)
Expect opposition in the business arena today, put on your most **inventive** diplomatic hat. **Partnerships** and relationships could **restrain you,** forcing you to compromise. Your usual talent for bright **ideas may be restricted,** possibly by authorities, or you **feel scattered.** Tomorrow's a better day.

OCT 26 OPPORTUNITY: SU-TRI-SU (OCT 25-27)
An excellent day for business activities. **Easy rapport with partners,** employees and authorities. **Schedule presentations, negotiations,** and conclude deals. You will be at your decision-making best. Opportunities will open for you. Be prepared to **take the bull by the horns.**

OCT 27 OPPORTUNITY: SU-TRI-MC (OCT 26-28)
Another favorable time for your career. **Rewards or a promotion, or a new project or partnership** may be approved. A perfect time to step into the public eye. Make a **speech or sales pitch,** or organize a **training.** Let the world know who you are today. Expect recognition for your **successes.**

OCT 29 CHALLENGE: SU-SQR-ME (OCT 28-30)
Possible **opposition** today, from **authority** figures. Your brain may not be functioning in its best form. Your communications, speaking, writing and thinking could run into **obstacles.** A good day to **work at the office,** or **delegate your projects** to others you can trust to say the right words.

OCT 30 OPPORTUNITY: SU-TRI-MO (OCT 29-31)
Today's a day to enjoy a sense of peace of mind. Be thankful for the gift of your relationships, home and family, as they support your efforts in the business world. Expect **opportunities to meet with clients, customers** and business associates. You benefit by expressing your gratitude for their support in the recent past. **Investment in real estate** and your home.

Notice that the *Opportunities* are the Trines and Sextiles, while the *Challenges* are the Squares and Oppositions. For example, October 20th's transit is "JU-SQR-PL," which is Jupiter squaring Pluto. The dates in parens cover the period of the transit's power.

The Astrology Of Successful Decision-Making

3. PREDICTING YOUR COMPETITION'S FUTURE DECISIONS

> **SUCCESS RULE #3:**
> LEARN TO PREDICT YOUR COMPETITION'S NEXT MOVES, THEN USE YOUR KILLER INSTINCT TO CREATE AN ADVANTAGE IN THE MARKET. THINK WIN/WIN, BUT WIN!

In the preceding Step Two, "The Right Timing," we focused on predicting *your* future as an individual person based on *your* transits.

Here in Step Three, you'll focus on predicting the likely future actions of your competitors, plus some astrological guidelines for your counter-moves.

Let's face it, aside from forecasting of your own future, the single most important use of astrology, economics, technical market analysis or any other forecasting strategies is in the ability to accurately predict the behavior of *other people,* individually and in large groups, especially the securities markets.

In the movie, *Back To The Future,* the lead character is able to make a fortune because he has *seen the future,* so when he goes back, he can anticipate it, control it and *then change his destiny and fortunes!*

That's basically what every economist, investor, trader and astrologer is trying to do ... *anticipate the future and get there ahead of the crowd!*

This requires some gut instincts about mass psychology.

First, let's examine this competitive drive as the 21st century paradigm shifts into the new astrology, and see what's already in progress, especially in the business of stock market trading. Let's see how *you* can profit by using astrology to predict the behavior of the individuals and the world around you.

PSYCHOLOGICALLY EVERYONE'S A STAR IN THEIR OWN WORLD!

Understanding the individual psychological drive to succeed and win is an essential beginning point.

Oh, the joy of winning! We love it.

The thrill of psyching out your opponent. Second guessing their next move. Strategies. Beating them to the punch. Knowing where the next pitch will be. Blitzing, sacking the quarterback. Forecasting a top in the market, selling off, and being right. Give me a high-five!

The *killer instinct,* the law of the jungle. It's inbreed, physiologically locked in our genes. Men have it. Women have it. We are all hunters.

It's stronger than the sex drive!

You can talk about the Olympic ideal of playing just to be in the game, but deep down the drive's there to collect the spoils of war - the checkered flag, a gold medal, the blue ribbon, the Lombardi trophy, the Stanley Cup, the World Series, or induction into the Hall of Fame.

Secretly, every fan has a fantasy ... they *are* Michael Jordan, or Wayne Gretzky, or Joe Montana. They *are* a star, a leader, a hero, a big winner. There are tens of millions of fans worldwide living out this fantasy.

Nobody understands this better than Budweiser, they invest hundreds of millions in the *killer instinct* every year.

This psychological *need to compete* drives our economy into the future.

You can talk "win-win" strategies in business negotiations, where everyone is supposed to win, but deep down the killer instinct is really saying, "okay, go ahead and talk all that win-win stuff ... *just so long as you win!*"

MONEY ASTROLOGERS: THE MICRO & MACRO PERSPECTIVES
Predicting the behavior of your competition requires a mathematical or scientific method of *anticipating* their future moves. To understand this, keep in mind that there as two related disciplines within this new astrological science:

Financial Astrologers: Stock & Commodity Market Trading. The first is used in a narrow segment of our total economic structure - the investing public. We call it financial astrology or *astro-trading.* This includes the specific methods used by all hyphenate-astrologers who trade in the stock and commodities markets, using astrological methods as well as charting, technical analysis and other methods.

Astro-Economists: Forecasting General Economic Behavior. Secondly, a more general approach to help you in anticipating the future behavior of your business competitors, in particular the general public. This is the profession of *astro-economics.* Here we will use astrology to create the H.E.R.D. index ("*Human Economic Reactive Decisions*"). This index is a measure the mass psychological tendencies influencing the general public as they make their collective decisions.

Many of the new Money A$trologers use both of these disciplines in their practices, out of necessity. W.D. Gann is an excellent example of this quality of genius.

TEXAN USES ASTROLOGY TO PREDICT THE "MADNESS OF CROWDS"

This basic human instinct drives every individual, and also drives the masses. In the last 100 years, beginning in the 1890's, mass psychology has become an important field of study, for advertising, politics and the stock markets.

In 1895, about the time J. P. Morgan's astrologer, Evangeline Adams, moved to New York City and started her career, a Frenchman, Gustav LeBon's published his classic on mass psychology, *The Madness Of Crowds*, one of the first in the field. LeBon's book focused attention on the herd instinct that drives mobs into action, creating trends and cycles in buying, selling and prices.

And while Morgan was helping Adams' kick off her astrological career, another young rising star, the mathematician-astrologer W. D. Gann, was also beginning his incredible career in the stock and commodities markets, building his fortune on charting cycles and trends.

The December, 1909 issue of *Ticker & Investment Digest* praised one month of Gann's trading, "During the month of October, 1909, Mr. Gann made, in the presence of our representative, 286 transactions in various stocks, on both the long and short side of the market. 264 of these transactions resulted in profits; 22 in losses. The capital with which he operated was doubled 10 times, so that at the end of the month he had 1000% on his original margin."

SUCCESS FACTS: Young William Delbert Gann, a transplanted west Texas farm boy, was just 31 years old at the time, working on Wall Street, without a computer, fax or copier. Yet his advisory letter sold for more than $3,000 *annually* back in those pre-World War I days when $15 was an average weekly wage. Gann virtually created the field of stock market charting, and in his lifetime revolutionized Wall Street, making over $50,000,000 during his life-time!

The Madness of Crowds was the psychological godfather of W. D. Gann's methods, which later evolved to become the *charting* or *technical market analysis* commonly used in today's stock and commodities trading. When plotted mathematically, these natural cycles and trends *rationalize* the behavior

PREDICTING YOUR COMPETITION'S DECISIONS

of the mob, thus you can create a picture of past trading habits on the stock exchanges - fluctuations in prices and volume - and hopefully, forecast and predict future turning points and events.

Another excellent book on the psychology of the stock markets is Donald Bradley's *Stock Market Prediction*. Bradley notes an "undeniable truth that business fluctuations seem too highly correlative with astrological factors to be the result of pure chance."

CHARTING MARKETS WITH ASTROLOGY: MOB RULE OR THE STARS?

From my perspective, there are two possible interpretations that could describe these key astrological cycles and turning points:

1. ASTRONOMICAL INTERPRETATION: COSMIC DETERMINISM?

The electromagnetic forces of the planets do in fact have a major affect on the human race as a whole, energizing human behaviors, causing or triggering predictable actions in large masses of people, thus creating future trends and cycles that can be forecasted and predicted.

2. PSYCHOLOGICAL MEANING: SELF-FULFILLING PROPHECY?

While accepting that interplanetary energies do exist, they are considered so faint that they have minimal effect.

Nevertheless, the *mere publication* of astronomical events and forecasts actually creates a mass "*psychological expectation*" in large numbers of people - the mob's response, the herd's reaction. After all, with over 27,500,000 working Americans *believing* in astrology, we can predict some powerful expectations, followed by a lot of *decisions and behaviors and actions about money!*

As a result, the mob's collective psyche *creates a self-fulfilling prophecy* out of the forecast, as the mob collectively reacts to these expectations. These behaviors can be tracked historically, and past trends can be mathematically projected, in order to predict the future. That's technical charting.

Of course both explanations are plausible. You cannot afford to discount either of them. Most probably there is an interactive, synchronistic relationship between the two interpretations.

In either case, some mathematical charting will improve your ability to predict future trends and increase your profitability!

THE KEY: *ALWAYS* USE OTHER FORECASTING TOOLS WITH ASTROLOGY

You can make astrology another important weapon in your arsenal as an entrepreneur and investor. However, it's important you to remember that even the experienced market traders and investor using astrology use it along with technical market charting of basic trends in their work. Astrological techniques help, but they normally combine astrology with other decision-making tools ... just like you might check with your accountant, your lawyer and your bankers for their opinions before making a decision.

Today, securities investors and market traders are the most sophisticated users of astrology as a predictive tool. However, astrology is *never* their sole decision criteria:

. **Arch Crawford,** the Wall Street Astrologer, explains that he tracks a total of 28 separate technical market indicators in his research, along with the astronomical events.

. **Larry Pesavento,** author of *Planetary Harmonics of Speculative Markets, Astro-cycles, The Trader's Viewpoint,* and a newsletter, *AstroCycles,* uses the

72 THINK ASTROLOGY & GROW RICH

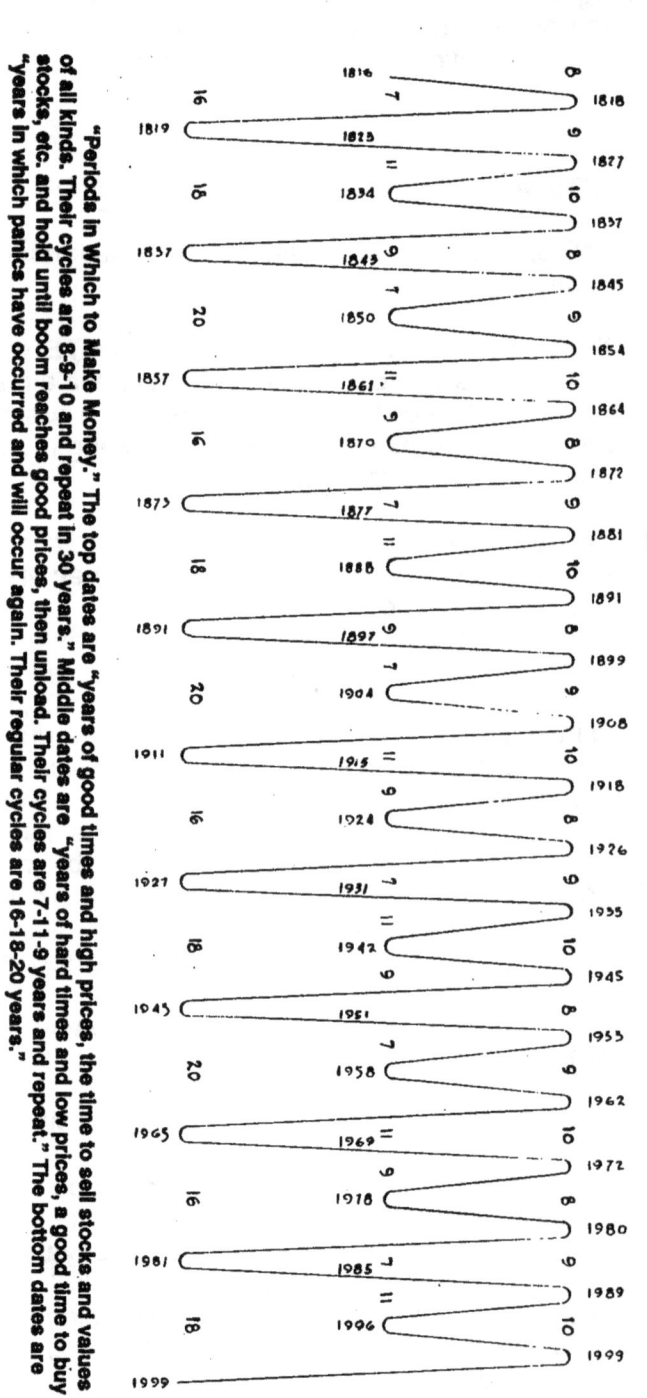

"Periods in Which to Make Money." The top dates are "years of good times and high prices, the time to sell stocks and values of all kinds. Their cycles are 8-9-10 and repeat in 30 years." Middle dates are "years of hard times and low prices, a good time to buy stocks, etc. and hold until boom reaches good prices, then unload. Their cycles are 7-11-9 years and repeat." The bottom dates are "years in which panics have occurred and will occur again. Their regular cycles are 16-18-20 years."

Source: Richard Mogey, Director, Foundation for the Study of Cycles, from his article "The Mystery of the 'Forecast of an Earlier Generation,' " in Cycles magazine, Summer of 1991. "Is Benner's forecast of any use to the cycles analyst? Overall, Benner's forecast has not performed too poorly. For example, he ... called for a panic in 1981, and the most severe recession since 1950 took place in 1982. Benner called for a top in 1989, another good call. He now is ... looking for a buying opportunity in 1996. This could be the end of the next major recession expected between 1994 and 1996. The next panic is due in 1999." The Foundation is an essential resource for information on business and economic cycles.

PREDICTING YOUR COMPETITION'S DECISIONS

Gilmore's WaveTrader in his commodity trades, as well as his own special techniques learned from over 20 years experience.

. **Jeanne Long,** the author of *Traders Astrological Almanac* and *Basic AstroTech*, also blends "the planetary energies, along with technical tools that work most consistently with astrological timing."

. **Carol Mull's** *Market Forecast* newsletter is "based on planetary aspects, cycles, Fibonacci ratios, Elliott Wave Theory, Gann Techniques, and my own original research." Mull is an author of two books with the charts of corporations, *The Standard & Poor's 500* and *750 Over-The-Counter Stocks*, which are used in the fundamental analysis of individual corporations.

CYCLES RESEARCH + ASTROLOGY = WALL STREET PROFITS
Today there are no *pure* astrologers in the financial markets, i.e., professionals using *only* the planets in making their decisions. The new Money Astrologers - astro-traders, astro-economists, financial astrologers and others using astrology in the business and financial world - *never* use astrology alone. They *always* combine their astrological information with other research on natural, business and economic cycles. Today's astrologers are really *cycles analysts* who use business, psychological & other natural cycles, *including astronomical data*.

In *Financial Astrology For The 1990's,* Long summarizes this relationship between technical analysis and astrology:

"Technical tools, therefore, allow you some element of control. (Not control over the markets, only control over yourself.) You can never tell the market what to do; you always let the market tell you what it is up to. Then with your technical tools, you monitor the action. It all boils down to *pattern recognition*.

"Restated, the technical tools monitor price and set up a framework within which the prices will fluctuate. *Planetary tools, however, give the timing for reversals of price.* When combined, these tools allow you to see the dance (visual patterns) and hear the beat (planetary timing) and therefore stay in tune with the market ... Do not take planetary signals without confirmation from technical signals." *Never.*

SUCCESS TIP: You know that the methods of Gann, along with those of his astrological and technical analyst disciples, may have had their *roots* in pure astrology a hundred years ago. But today, their *wings* are definitely in the 3 M's: *Market cycles, Mathematics and Mass psychology.* Today, global economic behaviors, statistical probabilities, life-style demographics, psych testing & hi-tech computer software are the tools of the new Money Astrologer.

INDIVIDUAL ASTROLOGY vs. BUSINESS & FINANCIAL ASTROLOGY

Can you use any astrologer help you make *business* decisions? Unlikely. Why? Because there are vast differences in the talent and experiences of astrologers, just as there are with physicians or attorneys.

"Many astrologers who are otherwise competent make the mistake of assuming that they can take their knowledge of traditional astrology and transfer it comfortably into the world of business and finance," according to Tim Bost, a financial astrologer, writing in Noel Tyl's book, *The Astrology of Crisis*.

"They often become frustrated when they discover they are *working with a different set of rules* and that traditional astrology doesn't always work as well as they would like it to in the financial arena ... These apparent shortcomings may be due to the fact that *a crisis for one person may be an opportunity for another*."

> **THE CONFLICT: ASTRO-PSYCHOLOGY vs. FINANCIAL ASTROLOGY**
>
> **PSYCHOLOGY AND ASTROLOGY:** The driving force behind modern astrology, Carl Jung, once said, "The great events of world history are, at bottom, profoundly unimportant. The essential thing is the life of the individual. This alone makes history, here alone do the great transformations take place." His approach is individual and very personal, in contrast to the traders.
>
> **ECONOMICS AND ASTROLOGY:** On the other hand, the market traders are more impersonal, like computers. "There is nothing mysterious about my predictions. If I have the data, I can use algebra and geometry and tell exactly by the theory of cycles when a certain thing is going to occur again," Gann is quoted as saying in "The Gann Technique," an article in *Financial Astrology For The 1990's* by Judy Johns, an astrologer and commodities broker.

The difference in approach is even more apparent when comparing the works of Larry Pesavento, an author, astrologer and successful stock and commodities trader, with the works of Stephen Arroyo, a gifted psychotherapist and an astrologer grounded in the work of Carl Jung.

The two focus on different planetary transits; Pesavento emphasizes the power of the *faster* ones in mass astro-psychological trends in the investing public, while Arroyo emphasizes the power of the *slower* planets in personal transformation:

"FASTER" PLANETS & FINANCIAL ASTROLOGERS. In *Astro-Cycles,* Pesavento says, "Remember, W.D. Gann said 'the faster moving planets are the key' and Saturn and Uranus move very slowly." The Moon cycles in 28 days. Mercury takes only 88 days to orbit the Sun, and during each cycle it will make major aspects to the other key planets over 100 times. The Moon, Venus and Mars also add a lot of aspects, intensifying their influence, power and, therefore, the probability of a turning point on any particular day.

"SLOWER" PLANETS & INDIVIDUAL ASTROLOGERS. Arroyo said, "you could throw out all the rest of astrology and just using Jupiter and Saturn ... have such a *practical* tool that it would be better than any other method [in dealing with the cyclical] nature of important developments, changes and growth periods in your life." Jupiter and Saturn take *12 and 29 years* respectively to complete a revolution of the Sun, and make fewer aspects than the other planets. Williams also used the Jupiter-Saturn cycle in *Astro-Economics.*

WHAT'S YOUR FOCUS: PERSONAL DECISIONS OR MASS BEHAVIOR?

Moreover, because the financial astrologers are more concerned with *mass psychology,* they are not normally interested in natal astrology or the birth astrology of the *individual,* only with *collective reactions* to overall astrological phenomenon that influence the general public. They come from two distinctly unique philosophical centers giving more importance to one end versus the other in the phrase, *the psyche is the cosmos.*

Elsewhere Gann summarized his strong belief in the power of the masses and the universe, "every class of phenomenon, whether in nature or in the market, must be subject to the universal laws of causation, harmony and vibration." Obviously Gann's astrology is in marked contrast to Jung's approach.

In summary, the psychologically-oriented astrologers focus more on the slower-moving planets, while the financial astrologers tend to look for their turning points using the fast-moving planets as benchmarks. In addition, their philosophies of life may well be as far apart as the planets they tend to work with, suggesting you be cautious in selecting your astrologers. You should also see the appendices for a checklist on how to pick an astrologer.

YES, THE MARKET DOES TRADE at ASTROLOGICAL TURNING POINTS!

Larry Pesavento's *Astro-cycles: The Trader's Viewpoint,* is an excellent resource in the field of financial astrology. As he notes at the outset, "I do not know the mechanism of *how or why* it works the way it does. However, I know what to do when I see the phenomenon unfolding." And indeed he does as a successful trader, which is why Pesavento's book is essential reading for any astrologer or trader in the stock market, possibly coupled with a day of private instruction with this expert.

He discusses his early discovery of Donald Bradley's book, *Stock Market Prediction,* which mentioned the aspects of **Venus and Uranus** influencing stock market prices. Pesavento then researched this astrological phenomena and concluded, "These aspects were so accurate as a short-term trading and timing device that they could be used in trading stock index futures ... it is the single most accurate short-term timing mechanism I have researched."

Pesavento's book reviews many specific aspects of the transiting planets, both fast and slow moving. Here are just a few examples of the key aspects creating major turning points in the markets:

SECRETS OF A SUCCESSFUL TRADER ... 90%+ ACCURACY!

. **VENUS-URANUS:** In an October 1990 *Trader's World* article Pesavento observes that further research on Venus-Uranus aspects tested "with over 90% accuracy in predicting short term stock market changes in trend!"

. **VENUS-PLUTO:** aspects of these two planets are "a powerful tool in timing gold and stock market transactions."

. **VENUS-JUPITER:** "a very strong relationship to the gold market."

. **MARS-JUPITER:** "very powerful and accurate," especially near lunar activity.

. **MARS-SATURN:** "very important to the timing of live cattle futures. It does not work with pork bellies."

. **JUPITER-SATURN:** In discussing the slower moving planets, he concludes, "It is my opinion that the Jupiter-Saturn aspects would be difficult to use in trading because of their long-term implications." However, the Jupiter-Saturn 20-year cycle is an accurate as a general indicator of long-term business cycles according to Lt.Cmdr. David Williams' observations in his book, *Financial Astrology.* Similarly, with Saturn-Uranus which is a 45 year cycle.

. **JUPITER-URANUS:** Interestingly, Pesavento notes the *medium* range aspects of Jupiter-Uranus (with a full synodal turn of 13.8 years from conjunction to conjunction) as another indicator of business cycles, noting the "All serious students of astrology have examined this cycle and have determined its ability to predict business activity. *Over 250 different types of economic data respond to this 41 month cycle phenomenon.*" The Foundation has even more information.

Astro-Cycles has a wealth of other information, including the "Ten Rules of Trading" and a "Cycles-Timing Analysis Sheet." Jeanne Long's *Traders Astrological Almanac* is another excellent resource. For some general reading on financial astrology, see Barbara Koval's *Time and Money, The Astrology of*

Wealth. Koval details many specific astrological guidelines for price changes and market trading, political and economic trends.

> **KEY MONEY-MAKING TOOL:** You should make special note of the fact that in researching the *Ephemeris*, the commodities trader Larry Pesavento observes that the average number of aspects on a given day is eight, and using a standard statistical deviation he advises that, "whenever you see a very small number of aspects (3 or less) or a very large number of aspects (14 or more) you can assume that something very dramatic is about to happen in the stock market." What a great tool to help an entrepreneur predict major economic turning points!

CAN THE DECISIONS OF 27,500,000 *WORKING* AMERICANS BE WRONG?

Now that we've seen the practical application of astrology in the stock and commodities markets, let's see how you can use this concept to your advantage and profit in the general world of business decision-making.

How can you *astrologically* "psych-out" your competition in the general business and economic worlds? First, consider that research studies show that 25% of all Americans "believe" in astrology. It influences their behavior; they go to astrologers, buy books on astrology, and follow their transits. And when a major planetary event is carried in the news (like a Mercury retrograde or the full eclipse of the Sun), a much larger percentage of the population becomes aware and may react by making economic decisions.

In short, today astrology is already part of the mindset of 25% of the American population, that's 27,500,000 employed Americans and a lot of economic power!

> **SUCCESS FACT:** *Time* magazine estimated, "50 million or so other Americans ... look at the alignment of the stars for guidance," in their extraordinary, seventeen page review of the impact of astrology on the Reagan Presidency, based on former Secretary of Treasury Donald Regan's book, *For The Record*.

It doesn't take much to start a trend on Wall Street, Main Street or Corporate America. Major trends are often decisions made by a mob, a herd, the masses. A little rumor leaks to the media, it grows bigger and you've got a stampede.

This phenomenon can be measured by the H.E.R.D. Index (*Human Economic Reactive Decisions*). Once the H.E.R.D.'s reaction begins, it builds on the increasing *psychological expectations* of the general public. Maybe they're not great decisions, but they're real ones, the collective decisions of a strong, silent *conspiracy*. We know the *H.E.R.D.* drives the business and financial world more than any *rational* decision-making processes, *and it can be predicted.*

HOW YOU CAN PREDICT THE COMPETITION'S NEXT DECISIONS

Keep in mind that your goal here is to develop decision-making strategies that allow you to successfully forecast the future behavior of other people ... either for an individual or for the business world as a whole.

The H.E.R.D. Index - a quasi-scientific system of quantifying what "they" (the rest of the world) are likely to do on a given day - is an astrological technique for predicting the macro-economic behavior.

Basically, you are comparing your particular transits to the general transits affecting the whole planet, en mass. You'll need a print-out of your daily transits and a print-out of the transits as they affect everyone on the planet. The H.E.R.D. index can be calculated quite easily, as you'll see on page 78.

PREDICTING YOUR COMPETITION'S DECISIONS

FIRST: WILL <u>YOUR</u> DAY BE AN "OPPORTUNITY" OR A "CHALLENGE?"

Let's build on the material in the last chapter on Rule #2. Suppose you have a important business meeting next week, say on Friday. Is next Friday a good day for you to have a meeting? Will *your* transits be *opportunities* or *challenges*?

Again, you must always start from your own center. That is, know the key characteristics of your natal chart. Then look at your transits report and check your daily transits (the angles between the current positions of the planets to the natal planets at the moment of your birth), using this formula. It takes a minute.

EXAMPLE: COMPUTING YOUR DAILY OPPORTUNITIES & CHALLENGES

In the sample Transit Forecast at the end of the last chapter each day had only one transit. When you have *more than one* transit use this technique:

1. ADD UP OPPORTUNITIES: mainly the 120 degree Trines and 60 degree Sextiles, and give each one 10 points (if you want to get fancy, instead of equal weights, you could weight the Trines at 8 points and 5 points for a *sextile*). For example, let's say you have 2 Trines and a Sextile today. That's +30 points.

2. SUBTRACT OUT CHALLENGES: primarily the 90 degree Squares and the 180 degree Oppositions. The sophisticated way says give 10 points to all Oppositions and 7 points to the Squares. Or simplify; give them both a minus 10 points. Let's say you have one Opposition and one Square. A minus 20 points.

3. FACTOR IN CONJUNCTIONS: place the Conjunctions in one or the other category, based solely on *your* gut instincts of their meaning after reviewing the interpretations in your computer print-out. You may make some mistakes, but like any learning process, you'll improve with experience. Assume you have one in the example. As a starter, *add* +10 points *(and see my note on page 80)*.

4. NET BOTTOM-LINE: is the net difference between the pluses and the minuses, the opportunities and the challenges noted above. In the example, you have 30 minus 20 plus 10 or a net of +20. You can handle these calculations in a few minutes, or just "eye-ball" them quickly.

Now, what's the prediction for that future date? Is it a good day for business and social contacts? Or a time to get caught up on back office work? Will it be a *hot day* dominated by opportunities, or a *cold day* filled with challenges?

"HOT" DAY ... A NET OPPORTUNITIES DAY FOR YOU: that is, did you decide or predict that a particular day in the future will be a net opportunity day for *you*, because *your* opportunities weigh more than *your* challenges? If so, it may be a great day for negotiating a contract, traveling or calling potential new clients, depending on the planets involved. Or is the day a cold one.

"COLD" DAY ... A NET CHALLENGES DAY FOR YOU: where *your* challenges weigh more than *your* opportunities? Where you should move more cautiously, double check documents, spreadsheets, flight schedules and the people around you?

In the above example, it would be a "hot day" for you, because you have more plusses than minuses.

It's that simple.

Several business clients tell me they informally calculate whether it's a hot or a cold day based on their *gut reactions* after reading their individual computer print-out, without going through any formal calculations, but the process is basically the same.

For now, keep it simple, while you get a feel for the process of evaluating your day in advance using *your* astrology, and don't worry about making mistakes, your *inner astrologer* will guide you.

SECOND: YOUR COMPETITION'S OPPORTUNITIES (AND CHALLENGES).

Now do the same thing with the general aspects made by the transiting planets as they affect *everyone on earth.* All you need is a copy of the *American Ephemeris 1991-2000* from the Astro Communication Services. Or, better yet, just buy any one of the easy-to-read astrological calendars available in any metaphysical bookstore. These calendars will tell you the key aspects each day.

THE H.E.R.D. INDEX: "HUMAN ECONOMIC REACTIVE DECISIONS"

The H.E.R.D. Index will help you estimate the public's psychological mood for today; will the larger world of competition be having a hot day or a cold day?

"HOT" DAY ... A NET OPPORTUNITIES DAY, where the opportunities add up to more than the challenges. An upbeat day for the business and consuming public. For those trading in the public securities markets, a time to be *bullish* and *buy*, or ...

"COLD" DAY ... A NET CHALLENGING DAY where the challenges exceed the opportunities, signaling that the public and the markets are likely to be in a *bearish* or *selling* mood. Odd events. A time for caution and discipline.

Now, in the same way as you just did with your individual transits, assign a weight to each of the transits listed in the ephemeris that day. Then add up the totals for the opportunities and subtract totals for the challenges. The net difference is the H.E.R.D. Index. This may tell you whether you're going to run into a bunch of optimists or pessimists when you get up in the morning.

Many days are that simple, and this is just one way to quantify each day astrologically ... or better yet, it is a a way to quantify the "*psychological expectations*" of the masses into a numerical index, the H.E.R.D. Index, especially if you're trying to plan something like an important *public* seminar.

Also, when you are gauging the likelihood of the day as a turning point, be especially mindful of the *number* of planetary aspects.

Although Pesavento is specifically examining the stock market for turning points in price trends, this advice also works as a gauge in the general world of business and economic activity. In the world of business and finance, you need to explore every possible *edge* to make money.

THIRD: KNOWING YOUR "POWER DAYS" ... YOU vs. THE WORLD.

Now you have an astrological *prediction* or, perhaps more accurately, a gut feeling of whether the day will be a day of *opportunities* or a *challenging* day for you, and you also have a similar prediction for the public at large.

This quasi-scientific process is a way of quantifying and adding structure to a process that I believe many executives and entrepreneurs *already use, naturally and instinctively.* We make judgments about having a *good* or a *bad* day all the time, for ourselves and for others. Since many people are already being influenced by astrology every day, you can now measure and use that knowledge to your advantage, in planning your decisions and actions.

Let's put it all together. Here is a decision-making model covering the four possible combinations:

PREDICTING YOUR COMPETITION'S DECISIONS

> **POWER DAYS: YOUR DECISIONS versus THE COMPETITION.**
>
> **1. BOTH YOU & THE HERD ARE "HOT:"** this should be a great time for action, you're moving toward opportunities in a supportive, favorable environment. A great time to plan meetings, presentations, negotiate contracts, meet the press.
>
> **2. YOU'RE "HOT" & THE HERD'S "COLD:"** I'd advise you to get into action, but expect to run into problem and obstacles. Be especially diplomatic, mindful of the opposition, expecting strange behaviors. A good time to be contrary and outfox the competition.
>
> **3. YOU'RE "COLD" & THE HERD'S "HOT:"** You may feel like sitting quietly and do nothing by yourself, possibly working in your office. Yet, if you do you may pass up some choice outside opportunities. Without pushing your own decisions, take advantage of what others have to offer.
>
> **4. BOTH YOU & THE HERD ARE "COLD:"** Make decisions and take action with considerable caution, you may be your own worst enemy in a hostile world.

DISCOVER HOW TO MAKE THE COMPETITION WORK FOR YOU!

Here's another way to summarize these astrological decision criteria. As you go through your day, whether you formally use a technique like the H.E.R.D. Index or just gauge it by *seat-of-the-pants hunches* and *gut instincts*, you are constantly making judgments about your competition. Thus, armed with a keen sense of "them" and their *astro-psychological expectations*, you can narrow your decisions down to one of three and thus focus your power during the day:

CONTRARIAN POWER ... When To *Go Against* The Herd: Be a contrarian. Leaders *create* trends, often by acting in a contrary manner, virtually creating something out of nothing. First, act on *your* transits, *your* gut hunches, and *your* mentors, especially if they show a direction contrary to what the masses are doing. Entrepreneurs do it all the time, find a need, fill it with your niche. Walt Disney was turned down by 300 banks before Disneyland was financed.

LEADING EDGE POWER ... When To *Flow With* The Herd: When you can't beat them join them, right. Wrong. Well, maybe sometimes. Whatever, just trust your instincts and transits, no matter what. Even when the herd seems to have all the cards stacked in their favor, never, *never* flow with the masses *unless* the decision resonates with your own center of power. If you decide to go along with the crowd, step in and lead the pack!

STAYING POWER ... When To *Sit Tight*, Do Nothing: There is a time for waiting. Waiting is not inaction, it is just *waiting*, letting the forces of nature work for you, preparing the way. Dr. Gunsaulus waited for two years before delivering his million dollar sermon. And while you're waiting, go to a seminar by a motivational speaker, like Tony Robbins, Les Brown or Wayne Dyer. Or reread *Think and Grow Rich*, it will rekindle your dreams of success and prosperity.

THE COMPETITIVE BOTTOM-LINE: TRUST YOUR INNER ASTROLOGER

The bottom-line rule is simple. You must *always* trust your own internal astro-gyroscope, the *inner astrologer*, whether you examine your transits and charts or not. You must *always* rely on *your* mission, *your* opportunities, *your* challenges, *your* second opinions. While it is important to predict the probable direction of the masses using astrology, in order to be able to plan your counter-moves or take advantage of your competitor's moves, *never fall into the trap of letting any mass astrological trends control your life!*

A TECHNICAL NOTE ON THE VALUE OF A CONJUNCTION

Some side comments about the evaluation of conjunctions are in order. If you want to simplify your work with the conjunctions, you can simply weigh *all of the conjunctions as opportunities*, giving them 10 points each in the above process. This would, of course, force or encourage you into making them *opportunities, no matter what*, and learning on the lessons of that transit. Generally, look at the conjunctions as *turning points, opportunities* for some people, *challenges* for others, make of them as you will. As one wise woman said, "one man's pleasure is another man's poison."

In *Astro-cycles, The Trader's Viewpoint*, Pesavento also adds support to the premise that, at least in the securities markets, the conjunctions are positives or opportunities; "Some aspects are associated with bullish action, and others with bearish price action. *Conjunctions* (0 degrees), *Sextiles* (60 degrees) and *Trines* (120 degrees) *are associated with strength in the market.* Squares (90 degrees) and Oppositions (180 degrees) are associated with weakness."

In evaluating conjunctions as either opportunities or challenges, if you do want to get more mathematically esoteric, refer to Carol Mull's excellent article, "Predicting The Dow," in *Financial Astrology For The 1990's*, or Bradley's *Stock Market Predictions* has an excellent section on "Estimating The Power of Aspects," although he seems to admit that the process is, in the final analysis, very much a subjective art because of the many factors involved.

The Astrology Of Successful Decision-Making

4. PICKING THE RIGHT PARTNERS & TEAMS

> **SUCCESS RULE #4.**
> **LEVERAGE YOUR POWER BY PICKING THE RIGHT TEAM,**
> **RIGHT PARTNERS, RIGHT RELATIONSHIPS, RIGHT NETWORK**
> Creating A Balance of Power in a Positive Support System.

J. Pierpont Morgan once advised his audience to "select not partners for money, but for talent and brains." Selecting the right partners and team is a crucial decision to your success. When two or more are focused on the same goals and supportive of each other, Napoleon Hill calls it a *master mind*.

We are social animals. Thus, you can leverage, magnify and amplify your personal power through other people, in your personal and working relationships. In other words, it's highly likely that you will fulfill your destiny and achieve your mission in life through partnerships and team-playing, and as a member of numerous business and social *organizations and networks*. This means working with your:

- family, lovers and friends,
- customers, clients and competitors,
- bosses and employee teams,
- attorneys, accountants and bankers,
- authorities, consultants, doctors and advisors,
- teachers, therapists, gurus and coaches,

and so many other kinds of business and personal relationships, partnerships and peer contacts. This means, delegating, hiring, partnering, joint venturing, sharing, networking, teaching, writing and many other methods of expanding your personal power.

The emerging new Money A$trology offers various excellent techniques for determining the compatibility of partners, employees and other members of the team. In general, these techniques represent the following basic three-step astrological process.

> **FIRST: BE SELFISH & FOCUS ON YOURSELF, SEPARATELY!**
> In other words, Know Thyself. Your Life-Cycle, Your Mission
> And Goals, Your Needs and Your Inherent Tendencies in Relationships.

Before you ever look at your partners' chart, you *must* understand "who you are" astrologically, *your* mission and *your* life-cycle. You must check out your chart *first* and develop a *written* profile of *your* ideal partners, before the matching process ever starts. Keep in mind the kind of strategic profiling that a business or executive search firm will do *before* beginning its search to hire the new partner, executive or employee.

In particular, the signs on your Ascendant and 7th House (the house of relationships) and any planets in those houses will reveal the special qualities you need in a relationship. Although other astrological factors do come to play, you can start by analyzing your *relationship axis*, the 180-degree *horizontal line* between your Ascendant or individual personality and your 7th house of relationships, which is directly opposite the Ascendant.

In addition, remember that *you are your own best astrologer.* Astrology is a projection or a reflection of your identity and personality. In the Jungian cosmology, what you are seeing and seeking in others is really a part of yourself, maybe your alter-ego, your Shadow side, or your Higher Self, for example. When in doubt, listen only to this *inner astrologer*, it must override the advice of any professionals or reports.

> **SECOND: FOCUS ON YOUR PARTNER AS A SEPARATE PERSON.**
> **Know Your Partner's Life-Cycle, Their Life Mission And Goals,**
> **Their Needs, And Their Capacity For Relationships.**

Look the other individual's chart, and go through the same method of interpretation just completed on yourself. In a way you'll be reading between the lines of their resume!

"Where are *they* coming from?" What is *their* mission in life? What is *their* capacity for *relationships in general*? What goals have *they* targeted? What are the major issues facing them in *their* current life-cycle. Where and when can you predict *their* challenges and conflicts, as well as *their* opportunities for personal, economic and spiritual growth.

If you fully understand your own chart, you will be close to *intuitively* knowing whether someone else's chart *fits* yours ... that's *creative* astrology in action.

> **THIRD: NOW, FOCUS ON THE WHOLE RELATIONSHIP.**
> **Review The Compatibility Ratios For Matching The Partners.**

After you separately analyze and interpret the charts of the individuals involved (or in the case of a business, you would be matching a potential new executive, partner or employee to a predefined *ideal* profile), you are ready to run a full diagnosis of *the match itself:*

How do the two of you fit together, is this a positive, supportive relationship? In a business organization or a professional firm such as a law partnership, is this the best person for the position? How will their personality work with the others on the team?

Here are a few books describing the primary methods used in compatibilities; Arroyo, *Relationships & Life Cycles,* Abadie & Bader, *Love Planets,* Forrest, *Skymates,* and March & McEvers, *The Only Way To Learn About Relationships.*

THE TWO MAIN METHODS OF TESTING PARTNERS' COMPATIBILITIES

These books will describe in more detail the two main astrological methods of testing the compatibilities of relationships and partnerships:

A "COMPARISON" OF THE TWO INDIVIDUAL CHARTS: this method of comparing two charts is referred to as "synastry." On comparing one-to-one relationships, the planets of one person are placed on the other's chart, with all their planets located in one of their charts. This is probably the one technique most frequently used in analyzing relationships.

One method of analyzing these partnerships simply looks at the compatibilities of the *signs* of just five astrological powers - the Sun, Moon, Venus, Mars and the Ascendant. Others will focus on the *angles or aspects* between the two partner's planets. Either way it means checking the areas of *opportunity* versus the *challenges* in a way similar to what we discussed earlier.

THE POWER OF TEAMS & PARTNERS

While the calculations are not overly complicated, the art of interpreting these comparisons requires practice. So you are well advised to consult with a specialist in this field of astrology.

A NEW ASTROLOGICAL "COMPOSITE" CHART: the second major astrological technique used in relationship analyses requires the calculation of a third chart that blends the two people together, the *composite* chart. First, you calculate the midpoints between each of the planets of the two individual charts, i.e., if your sun is at 10 degrees Taurus and mine is at 20 degrees Taurus, the midpoint is at 15 degrees Taurus. Then the new composite chart - the relationship's chart - is interpreted as a *single unity.*

COMPUTER-GENERATED RELATIONSHIP & PARTNERSHIP STUDIES

There are a number of inexpensive computer software programs that are commercially available to assist you with either of these methods, both in the calculations and analytical reports. Often I will do most of my interpretations looking at the compatibility grid highlighting the major aspects between the two sets of planets, and ask, *do the opportunities outweigh the challenges?*

However, don't expect the current computer programs to become your primary decision-making tool. They're not sophisticated enough to handle all the variables. Like a lot of psych tests used for similar purposes, they lack neat *yes/no* bottom-line answers. According to feedback from my clients, the reliability of many of these computerized compatibility reports is questionable, in part because of the many contradictions that tend to confuse rather than enlighten. They will, however, encourage dialogue in the selection process.

SUCCESS TIPS ON BUSINESS PARTNERSHIPS & TEAM-BUILDING

Stephen Arroyo, psychotherapist and astrologer, makes some interesting observations about compatibilities in his book, *Relationships & Life Cycles:*
"there are different kinds of compatibility, too. If you're doing a business comparison, you don't need such wide-ranging compatibility as ideally you would like to find in a marriage or in a living together relationship.

"If it's a business comparison, what you mainly look at are Saturn and Jupiter aspects, and Mercury; look at the communication - can they communicate with each other; Jupiter aspects often show whether you would be of benefit to each other financially, as well as whether you really trust each other. Problematical Neptune aspects should also be examined because those can show all kinds of misunderstandings, deception, and what not.

"For business purposes, you should *still* analyze the complete comparison, but the sexual compatibility, for example, with your business partner would be unnecessary. You don't need the Sun and Moon things [harmonious aspects between the two sets of Suns and Moons] to be quite so compatible either, although it can certainly help the relationship."

Relationships are one of the great mysteries of life. I strongly recommend that with any serious opportunity - intimate or business - you get the advice of a professional counselor, relying on the computer reports *only* as a starting point.

FINANCIAL & BUSINESS PARTNERSHIPS: A SIMPLER ANALYSIS

In business situations, the selection of key employees and executives is obviously a very important process. Therefore, I would also recommend and assume that business clients using the astrological compatibility studies would be doing it *in conjunction with* some time-honored psychological and related types of testing procedures; *Personal Profile Systems,* Performax Systems International, the personality types in *The Enneagram*, or the *Meyers-Briggs Type Indicator,* a psychological test based on Jung's structure of personality.

When you have the right information about a potential partner, executive or key employee, you can then blend their astrological compatibilities along with any psychological testing available.

BUSINESS SUCCESS & "THE POWER BEHIND YOUR THRONE."

Intimate relationships are more complex to interpret than business partnerships. My first exposure to the whole business of astrological compatibilities was very enlightening. I first tried the simple methods outlined by five different astrologers, checking out how I fared with the six major intimate relationships of my earlier life. *Not one of those six fit the profile for any of my ideal relationships in any one of the five systems.* Moreover, I had never even dated anyone in some of the very favorable categories. After that I began taking the astrology of partnerships much more seriously.

> **SUCCESS TIP: LOOK FOR THE NET OPPORTUNITIES VS. CHALLENGES**
> In analyzing the "fit" of a relationships, intimate or business, you will find some interesting mathematical systems used in weighting all the astrological factors, such as Abadie and Bader's book. Generally, they break all factors into one of two classes:
> . JOINT OPPORTUNITIES, the favorable aspects and/or the relationships between signs get mathematical points *added* to a total because they're considered positive and supportive, and
> . JOINT CHALLENGES, unfavorable aspects and signs will get points *subtracted* from the total because they imply potential problems.
> . NET SUMMARY, the net of the two above is the bottom-line summary of your astro-analysis. Actually, this is the bottom-line of any astrological relationship or partnership study, for personal or business purposes.

Most of these systems focus specifically on the angular relationships of the inner planets - your Sun, Moon, Venus, Mars, plus the Ascendant. Many of these systems also examine the angles between Jupiter and Saturn to the five inner planets. In *The Book of Lovers,* Carolyn Reynolds, suggests that you look for a partner whose Moon sign is the same as your Sun sign and whose Sun sign is the same as your Moon, as a simple method of compatibility. Some experience of your own plus the aid of a good astrologer working with you will make this process smooth and productive.

THE BOTTOMLINE: POWER IN RELATIONSHIPS, PARTNERSHIPS & TEAMS

In spite of the current state-or-the-art and the limitations of the computer analyses, I've discovered that they are quite valuable as communication devices, jumping off points that encourage discussion about the main relationship issues in business and personal relationships.

Moreover, these systems can be extremely helpful, when used in conjunction with third-party reality checks with friends, therapists and astrological counselors who can be counted on for honest feedback in the appraisal of a romantic relationship during the starry-eyed first 100-day honeymoon.

We all need relationships, intimate partners as well as business partnerships. If you leverage yourself right, your personal power will increase greatly, because *the people around you really do want to help you achieve your goals.*

The Astrology Of Successful Decision-Making

5. PICKING THE RIGHT LOCATIONS & MARKETS

> **SUCCESS RULE #5.**
> **LOCATE YOUR BEST GEOGRAPHIC POWER BASE,**
> **TARGET THE RIGHT MARKET NICHE, THEN MAKE A POWER MOVE,**
> **Either Relocate There ... or Capitalize On Your Existing Location!**

Where *should* you locate your *power base*? If you want to maximize the possibility of achieving your mission in life, what's the best place for you? This question is rarely asked when the person *intuitively* knows that where they are now is the best place to be.

Astrological relocation studies can be quite valuable in certain cases and under certain conditions:

1. When the study is viewed primarily as a "creative whack on the side of the head," to help you think through your natural decision-making processes, and

2. As a "second opinion" to a review of your mission statement and current life-cycle transition, possibly with your company's business plan.

Otherwise they should be used with considerable caution, *and never used as a first opinion or as the only opinion.*

This astrological technology is relatively new, made possible by the introduction of computers into the field of astrology in the 1970s. In its present level of development, however, these astro-locality studies can be somewhat limiting and misleading, as we'll see below, especially if they are not integrated into an overall analysis of the whole person and all their transits.

Moreover, the state of the art with astro-locality research tends to focus on a "Johnny-one-note" approach, with primary emphasis the one or two key planets whose main axes cross a particular location on the planet. The process misses some of the subtleties of the angles the *other key planets* make to that location.

AN EXAMPLE: PARTNERS IN SEARCH OF A "POWER BASE"

An example will both show you some of the problems and illustrate a successful procedure for analyzing relocations.

A few years ago I completed several astrological consultations for a graphics arts entrepreneur and his wife, a computer programmer with a major corporation. Several months went by and then around Thanksgiving they asked me to come in and review some astro-locality maps which they had earlier purchased from a national supplier when considering a possible relocation.

They explained that she had been offered a promotion back East with her company. However, he said he was thinking about relocating his business activities in the Phoenix. They even mentioned a possible break in the marriage. I could feel the tension over the phone.

THE 5-STEP ASTROLOGICAL PROCESS OF "RE-LOCATION"

Their relationship was at a highly explosive moment in time, so I came prepared with five different astrological studies for each partner:

> **EXAMPLE: A COMPLETE 5-STEP "RE-LOCATION" ANALYSIS**
>
> **FIRST. NATAL CHARTS & GOALS**: I reviewed their individual birth charts, to refresh my memory about their personalities types, life missions and goals based on their astrological profiles.
>
> **SECOND. UP-COMING TRANSITS**: I checked their upcoming transits. Turns out both had several very heavy, challenging transits that coincidentally were peaking in a couple months, shortly after the New Year.
>
> **THIRD. PARTNERS COMPATIBILITIES**: next, I reviewed my compatibility study of them as a partnership, which was quite favorable.
>
> **FOURTH. GENERAL ASTRO-LOCATION MAPS**: *After* reviewing the individuals and their compatibilities, I then reviewed the astro-locality reports and maps they had bought from an astrological computer services company.
>
> **FIFTH. ASTRO-LOCATION CHARTS**: Finally, I used my own astro-locality approach and ran of new birth charts for each of them, to test each of the three of the locations they were considering. The method assumes that you are born at *precisely the same moment,* but on a different location on the planet. As a result, all the planets remain in the almost the same positions, however, the Ascendant, Midheaven and Houses rotate. Then I can analyze the impact of *all* the planets would have on a relocation, given the new house positions. More importantly, I can then estimate the effects a move might have on their success profiles using Dr. Gauquelin's astrological research.

Perhaps this was overkill, but I wasn't sure what to expect in their negotiations and I wanted to be fully prepared. And besides, it pushed me to totally re-examine the best way to use astro-locality studies in an overall astrological analysis.

When all the information was reviewed, it was apparent that there were some strong astrological reasons for this couple to live and work back East, *separately and together.*

After a couple hours the tension began to subside. Then the eye-opener came ... at the end of the session. The man admitted that he was avoiding going back East *because* he had an earlier astrologer tell him that he would be *invisible* back East, based on an interpretation of the astro-locality maps!

He had been hypnotized by that irresponsible remark. Fearing the accuracy of this "prediction" of his future, and his potential loss of identity, he had been seriously considering a separation from his wife!

ASTRO-RELOCATION: THE STATE OF THE ART & TECHNOLOGY

This experience convinced me that any astro-locality and relocation studies must be used only as a "second opinion" to a basic astrological reading for the person, but *never* as a solo decision-making tool. In addition, they should be part of an overall business or personal relocation analysis.

Remember, there are no inherently "good" or "bad" transits, or times, or locations, or charts. They are only road-maps to guide you. You must still make the decisions. You are responsible for your destiny.

THE POWER OF MARKETS & LOCATION 87

There is available several software suppliers and reporting services that print these astro-locality maps. The technology is generally based on Dr. Michel Gauquelin's research findings that emphasize the importance of the two major axes, the Midheaven and the Ascendant. Thus, in simple form, your bottom-line goal in making an astro-relocation decision is to shift the planets on your birth chart so that they move into more favorable positions, Gauquelin's *Power Zones*. Your birth *time* is exactly the same, you merely assume a new "birth" *location*.

In summary then, there are three main methods for astro-locality analyses:

THREE POPULAR METHODS OF ASTROLOGICAL RE-LOCATION

1. ASTRO*CARTO*GRAPHY: which is explained in Lewis and Guttman's *The Astro*Carto*Graphy Book of Maps*. This book is one of the best introductions to the subject of astrological relocation analyses and is particularly fascinating because it includes the relocation maps for many existing celebrities and historical figures.

Basically these maps include lines showing where each of the planets make aspects to your Ascendant and Midheaven. Astro-locality maps can be purchased with interpretations through either Jim Lewis' organization or Matrix Software. Astro Communications Services also has a similar astro-location map service, and Matrix even sells some of the software.

2. "LOCAL SPACE" MAPS: show the planets mapped as directions from your birthplace, allowing you to see what powers are emphasized depending on the direction your life takes, geographically and otherwise.

Matrix sells software for this purpose. In addition, Matrix Software is also marketing a new super-program called PRIMA which was developed by two Russian geniuses, Bogdanov and Lobenko. For a few hundred dollars you can have this versatile program that does a variety of astro-locality functions as well as the basic calculations for natal and transit astrology, compatibilities, and so much more. With this program you can test any location you desire quickly, although you must still interpret the data.

3. RELOCATION BIRTH CHARTS: as explained before, you can astrologically test new cities simply by recalculating your birth chart for the same exact time while using the proposed new locations and comparing the pros and cons of the new *house* positions of your planets. While it takes more time, this is the preferred method because it allows for a more comprehensive analysis of the individual and the relocation.

Again, I remind you that these astro-location analyses work great as *second opinions only*. Regardless of the methods you use, it is assumed and recommended that you have other astrological, business and personal motivations for considering relocation. As an astute astrologer once said to me, "*Know where you're going, don't just run away from where you are.*"

ACTION: EITHER RELOCATE ... OR STAY & RE-COMMIT!

Shortly after I ran into Joseph Campbell I began working on screenplays. By day Morgan Stanley still had my soul as an investment banker, but the artist in me started it's journey as a writer ... in the evenings, on weekends, during vacations, on airplanes, and in hotels during business trips.

I was anxious to move on to the new career. Yet, for three years my astrologer, my guru and my therapist all said, "wait, the moment isn't ripe, you will know when it is time." Finally, I got a telegram offering me a fellowship at the American Film Institute. The next day I resigned. The timing was right, I knew it in my heart. I had sent a signal out to the universe, an application to AFI. And after a delay, I got a message back from the universe. But I had made the initial decision to consider going to Hollywood.

YOUR BIGGEST "RELOCATION" IS PSYCHOLOGICAL *NOT PHYSICAL*

Normally, a relocation analysis is *not* a free-form process that, *in a vacuum*, picks out the very best place for you to live of *all possible locations on this entire planet.* There are always some limitations to our freedom and many of them may not be apparent to your astrologer.

A more general survey of the whole world may be exciting if you really are in von Oech's *Explorer* stage, and you may even uncover a few ideas you hadn't previously considered, but for the most part, people use this kind of analysis as a *second opinion,* to double-check their gut instincts about moving to a new location. And again, I caution you to make sure you look closely at your natal chart and transits along with the astro-locality studies.

You might try this rule: first select a few preferred locations based on your more important personal and business values. Then test those locations, astrologically as well as other techniques.

BOTTOM-LINE: USE ASTRO-RELOCATION FOR SECOND OPINIONS *ONLY*

Finally, while I have found the science of astro-locality helpful as a counseling tool, I am not convinced, either philosophically or physiologically, that we can alter a person's destiny astrologically *merely* by shifting their location *after their birth.* Their destiny and their future will unquestionably be altered, but not *merely* because of repositioning astrological energies.

If Jung's concept of synchronicity means anything, then our DNA/genes determined the time and the place to be born, not the planets. We chose the one location and time most appropriate for our mission this lifetime. I am not fully convinced that a new location would reverse or alter our birth decision and make any changes in our DNA/genes or our thought processes, etc. Obviously, a new location will result in some changes in the interplanetary electromagnetic energies we get from the transiting planets, but we remain the same person we were are birth, with the same inherited genes.

Notwithstanding the current state of the art and inherent limitations in this process, I invariably find these maps useful in counseling people, because they serve as a perfect *creative whack on the side of the head,* to force out some creative thinking from the deep recesses of the person's psyche.

SUCCESS TIP ... IF YOU DECIDE NOT TO MOVE TO THE NEW LOCATION.
Once you do complete your astro-locality analysis, you must make a conscious decision: cease all the soul-searching, get off the fence ... you must now either get into action and relocate, or *make a renewed commitment to your existing location and make the most of every day right where you are, taking full responsibility for making your present location the best place for you!*
Your natal birth chart is your main power tool and first line of offense, use it aggressively. When the chips are down, you will capitalize on your inherent powers in *any* location and create profitable opportunities.

The Astrology Of Successful Decision-Making

6. RISK MANAGEMENT & SECOND OPINIONS

> **SUCCESS RULE #6.**
> ALWAYS GET A SECOND OPINION TO MINIMIZE YOUR RISKS
> & MAXIMIZE YOUR SUCCESS ... ALWAYS.
> No Matter What Your Issues & Who Your Experts!

Astrologers make mistakes, many mistakes. So do economists, attorneys, cardiologists, nuclear physicists, and even cabdrivers. Their clients occasionally wind up in recessions, jails, cemeteries, black holes and dead ends.

Predicting the future is a tough business. Yet many risk it. Luckily, a few learned what my grandfather often told me, "the worse mistake you can make is to make the same mistake twice." As a great philosopher once said, "if you don't learn the lessons of history, you'll be forced to repeat them."

This chapter is about how can you improve your edge in forecasting your life and the world around you. Marilyn Ferguson notes in *The Aquarian Conspiracy*, that the key to transformation, to creative thinking solutions, to weathering the paradigm shift and coming out smelling like roses, *is problem-finding, not problem-solving.* Once you know what the problem is, the solution is usually obvious, *the answer is in the question.*

YOUR INNER POWER: LOVE-STRUCK OR STAR-POWER?

In one episode of *Magnum, P.I.*, the lead character is racing his Ferrari along the Hawaiian highways. We hear his inner dialogue, "Someday I'll write the book on how to be a successful private investigator," he says, and "Rule #1 is you always listen to that still small voice."

Above all else, trust *your* inner voice. Ignoring your *inner astrologer* can become quite costly as you'll see in the following example.

A few years ago a reputable astrologer, a friend of mine, started dating a successful real estate investor, a very bright guy trained as an accountant. Turns out he's been to Vegas three times in his life and won every time, between $8,000 and $23,000. He was great with numbers under pressure, he had some strong gut instincts, and they served him well.

She decided she could *improve* on his performance. So she got a computer print-out of his gambling transits for both downtown Vegas and The Strip. Yes, you can get them and they cover the timing for different games of chance.

Mind you now, she is an excellent astrologer with over 20 years in the business. But I could tell by her ambivalence that the lady wasn't at the top of her game with gambling astrology. Like asking a brain surgeon for advice about podiatry.

Off they went with their bankroll.

You guessed it. The next time I saw them he just shook his head. He had *lost* for the first time, luckily only a thousand. "Seems like every time my gut was telling me I was on a roll, she'd look at the computer print-out and tell me it's time to go somewhere else. It threw my instincts way off."

His *inner astrologer* gave him power. When the chips were down (literally), he should have trusted it and overridden the path of computer print-outs and the advice of the professional astrologer. Love got in his way. What's in yours?

You can't *bullet-proof* your decisions, but there are some time-honored methods and techniques that can help you, some super hi-tech, some ancient and some *new age*.

Let's look at some of these ways to reduce your risk exposure and increase your success potentials. You need an edge when you're in the middle of a major life turning point and are being *forced* to negotiate another *course correction* on the way to achieving your business and career targets.

FIRST: YOU SHOULD USE CONVENTIONAL METHODS & SOURCES.

In the first place, there are a number of non-astrological, left-brain resources that you would *naturally* use first in making business and career decisions. The left-brain is the rational half, often identified with science and males, while the right-brain is the intuitive, with the arts and women. Whole-brain decisions require the integration of both halves of your mental computer.

> **DECISION TEAM:** Without suggesting that you delegate your decisions to others, I still assume that *everyone* who sees an astrologer, or any other consultant, will also run the decision by a number of trusted advisors who can be relied on for some reasonably objective analysis based on their special expertise, and some honest, non-judgmental feedback. These may include:
> 1. Business partners and associates
> 2. Accountants, bankers and lawyers
> 3. Professional consultants in marketing and management
> 4. Mentors, therapists, gurus and coaches
> 5. Friends, loved ones and family members
>
> In real life, these people are more likely to be the initial opinions sought (after your own), with your second opinions coming from astrologers or some *new age* counselors, if at all. These *left-brain* advisors can do more for you than just input raw data. They are often an important sounding board, double-checking your own instincts, analysis and conclusions.

In making business decisions, astrological input is usually blended with other data, rather than used a sole basis for a decision. As Jeanne Long notes in her article, "New Concepts for Trading Commodities, "Do not take planetary signals without confirmation from technical signals." In short, get second opinions.

NEXT: TRY THESE 3 PROVEN ASTROLOGICAL TECHNIQUES

There are some practical astrological techniques that have been used for centuries to help men and women make important decisions. Kings and military leaders used them often to pick the best days to start wars, for example.

It's my opinion that these three techniques should *only* be used *after* analyzing the chart and transits of the primary decision-maker who will lead the action. However, I must admit that many astrologers have historically used these techniques by themselves, for the first and only opinion. In any event, the purpose of these astrological techniques is to increase the chances of a successful venture, whatever it is.

ONE: ELECTIONS - THE BEST TIME TO START A NEW VENTURE!

The *electional* technique is commonly used by many astrologers. This method helps you select the *best* times and dates to initiate projects, incorporate businesses, start a marketing campaign and any other new ventures, for example. This same basic method has long been used by physicians in picking the best dates for surgery.

Basically what you do is pick the best possible "birth moment" for a new venture, by avoiding unfavorable times and selecting the most advantageous of the remaining times available. As a result, the natal chart of the new venture will minimize the potentials for failure and give it the greatest possibility for success.

With the electional method, the new venture itself is treated like the birth of a human baby, except you have control over the exact time of birth. If this sounds a bit like planned parenthood and genetic engineering, you're right.

Computer programs are now available for electional decisions as well as horary astrology.

TWO: "HORARY" ASTROLOGY - THE ANSWER IS IN YOUR QUESTION

Here, the answer is in the question, literally. *Horary* astrological counseling, as it's called, has developed over the years as a method of answering all kinds of specific questions, ranging from careers, business and investment decisions, to relationship prospects, the location of lost items, the identity of criminals, and the timing of future events, to name a few.

The beauty of the *horary* process is that it is a fairly objective and almost mechanical process with a number of fixed decision criteria on how to come up with a simple yes/no answer, as well as more complicated decisions. Horaries are right-brain in premise and left-brain in procedure.

Although many astrologers use the horary technique for a first opinion, and sometimes the only opinion, I recommend that you use it *only* as a second opinion, in conjunction with an interpretation of the your personal transits. Otherwise, I would suspect that you didn't like the answers you got from your first opinion or the answers of your *inner astrologer*, so you're searching for a different and more favorable answer.

THREE: HOW TO ANALYZE THE SUCCESS OF AN EXISTING CONTRACT.

For everyone who's ever said, "This deal's my baby," a third astrological decision-making technique will have some personal as well as practical application. Just make sure you note the birth time of your "baby!"

This time-honored technique involves the analysis of a previously *signed* agreement or contract to predict the probability of a successful closing. It is often used with contracts of sale, real estate mortgages and investment financing agreements. The astrologer begins with the time the deal was signed and then interprets the chart for *that birth moment.*

While all three of these astrological techniques can be and are frequently used as solo decision-making tools, they work best when they are used as second opinions to an analysis of the decision-maker's natal chart and transits.

NEXT, TRY SOME ANCIENT DECISION-MAKING TECHNIQUES

Astrology is just one tool available to you. If your gut still doesn't feel right, there are many other forecasting tools to help you, *psycho-technologies* as Ferguson calls them in the *Aquarian Conspiracy*. Actually, if you're flexible and open, you'll try anything that triggers a *transformation* and a shift of consciousness into the whole-brain, anything that gets you out of your rut and into a new way of thinking, anything that brings about a personal paradigm shift!

If you feel you are not getting solid directions from either the conventional left-brain resources or from astrological resources discussed above, you may want to visit a master practicing one of the more respected ancient decision-making techniques, especially the Tarot cards, the I Ching and the Runes.

Keep in mind that each of these methods is intended to help you tap into *your own answers, from the power within you.*

BRAINSTORMING TOOL ... WHACKY SOLUTIONS TO YOUR PROBLEMS

You should also try a *modern* executive's version of these ancient techniques, Dr. Roger von Oech's "Whack Pack." The Pack is a creative decision-making tool designed to help you get unstuck, and out of the rut you're in. He created a unique deck of 64 cards based on his *creative thinking* system, one that will "allow you to look at what you're doing in a fresh way. ... It consists of 64 different strategies. Some highlight places to find new information. Some provide techniques to generate new ideas. Some lend decision-making advice. And some give you the 'kick' you need to get your ideas into action."

Get the Whack Pack! Try shuffling the deck, take a card, any card, and then meditate on it, play with it, etc. You just may discover in it the answers that the universe and your *inner astrologer* has wanted for your highest good all along.

He also suggests using the *Wall Street Journal* or the telephone directory's Smart Yellow Pages in the same way as the Tarot or Whack Pack, as a *random access* resource to *draw out of you the answer already within you.* The process is simple: randomly pick a page number, pick a column, then pick a sentence or word, and work with it ... that word contains the answer to your question.

Another often used *psycho-technological* resource is, of course, the psychic. There are some truly great psychics, such as Edgar Cayce. However, there are so many charlatans in that field I suggest you select one with extreme caution. I have discovered that many are merely using a form of Neuro Linguistic Programming, that is, reading your *body language* and feeding back your wishful thinking, giving you the answers they feel you want to hear. Unfortunately, you and they may even believe you're getting valid information about the future.

Yes, there are some excellent, credible psychics out there, but you need to do your *due diligence,* getting solid recommendations from people who have already used them, then question everything they say, leave nothing to chance, record everything, and in the end, trust your own instincts over their directions.

WHEN *NOTHING* YOU'RE DOING WORKS ... ZEN WATTS!

If you're still hesitating and confused, in a quandary, a dilemma, immobile, dead in the water, pause.

When nothing still *feels right*, perhaps you should just trust that feeling. Often I've advised uncertain people; "When in doubt, *don't.*" Don't do *anything*. Nothing. Trust that little voice that says, "It's not time, or that's not the way."

On the other hand, how do you know that these voices are not just your old fears from the past, that have stood between you and your dreams for decades?

When do you *feel the fear and do it anyway,* as Susan Jeffers advises in her book by that title? When do you *stop* listening to the still small voices within, because they just might be your mom or dad talking, and you can't trust them.

ZEN: SOMETIMES "DOING NOTHING" *IS* THE BEST SOLUTION.

Many people sit on fences, immobile, vacillating between legitimate intuitions that counsel them not to act now, and mental blocks that make them their own worse enemy.

When all else fails, how do you get past your double bind?

Zen may provide your answer. As Alan Watts says in *The Way of Zen*, "Sitting quietly, doing nothing, spring comes and the flowers grow."

Meditate on it. Perhaps using your natal chart and transits. Ask your *inner astrologer* for advice. Meanwhile, things will eventually work out on their own.

If *everything* you're doing really is bombing, maybe that's a signal from the cosmos that there really is nothing for you to do ... and it's time to stop trying, time to accept life on its own terms.

In Napoleon Hill's book, *Think and Grow Rich,* Dr. Gunsaulus waited for two years without taking action, *before the spirit moved him at the right time, for him.* Sitting quietly, doing nothing, his spring finally came. At the right moment, when he sprang into action, the Universe sprang into action *totally supporting him.*

OR, DO WHAT'S IN FRONT OF YOU: Yet another spiritual leader advises, "*I never just sit and do nothing* while waiting for God to tell me what to do. Rather, I do whatever is in front of me to be done, and I leave the results up to God; however it turns out, that's God's will for me." What's happening is supposed to be happening. Trust life, no matter what. Trust this thing called you.

SUCCESS STRATEGY - START *CREATING* PROBLEMS

Remember, sometimes "no decision" really *is* the best decision. As Marilyn Ferguson, author of *The Aquarian Conspiracy,* emphasizes in one of her tapes, the key to your transformation is probably not in being a great problem-solver or even a good decision-maker.

The key is in *asking the right questions,* in discovering which problems to work on, in pointing out problems previously ignored or denied ... and in becoming a rebel and a *problem-creator!*

OR, JUST DO *ANYTHING*: Get into action. Make some mistakes ... you just might hit a home run. At the least, you'll get some experience. After all, a guy batting *only* .300 in the major leagues is probably making a million bucks a year, even though he's making mistakes seven times out of every ten at bats!

OR, SURRENDER & LET GO. If doing something doesn't feel right, it's time to let go. Your decision's probably premature. Life is an unfolding mystery. So, trust your inner voice. Take a breather. Go for a short walk on the beach. *The answers will come.* The universe is trying to tell you to slow down, accept reality and flow with it for the moment.

An American was at a tea ceremony with a Zen master. The master poured the hot tea into his cup until it began running over the top, onto his hand, spilling on the floor. "Stop, stop, what's going on?" The master answered, "Your mind is like this cup, before new information can come in, you must empty it first."

OR, ESCAPE FROM IT ALL. Many psychologists, tough-minded business partners and friends may say you're just running away from your problems and remind you that you'll just carry them with you ... that *you can't escape from you.* True, but so what. Sometimes you need a break, it's the best *medicine* for you!

When the pressure's too great and the mind is resistant take a break.

Maybe a sabbatical, maybe a long weekend, maybe a walk for a cup of coffee. Anything to forget about it. Get away. Clear the mind, take a trip to the Big Sur, Sedona, Taos, Sundance, or the Catskills. Open your mind for some new information.

A few years ago I made friends with a New York gem importer visiting the Esalen Institute with his wife, a jewelry designer. Radically new designs started to flow from her while sketching next to a small creek. When they got back to the Big Apple I heard they had created a whole new line of jewelry art!

If you are in a dilemma about a decision and nothing's working, run away from it. I'm serious, get far, far away.

OR, LAUGH IT OFF. Please, have some fun. Stop being so serious, it's only your life. Norman Cousins used *The Three Stooges* and other classic comedies while recovering from cancer and a heart attack. Go to the Comedy Store!

Remember the advice in Roger von Oech's book, *A Kick In The Seat Of The Pants*, "The artist believes that there is a close relationship between the *ha-ha* experience of humor and the *aha!* experience of creative discovery. If you can laugh at something, then you're more likely to challenge the rules ... and look at it in unusual ways," and develop unique, innovative solutions. In other words, you make better decisions when you're having fun! *Seriously.*

THE BOTTOM-LINE: ALWAYS GET A SECOND OPINION ... YOURS!

In *Grow Rich With Peace of Mind,* Napoleon Hill said, "know your own mind, live your own life." Remember, *all opinions are second opinions, except yours! You* create the question, you decide whose opinions you'll accept, and you must make the final decision.

Yes, I encourage you to *always get a second opinion* - from a business professional, friend or spouse, from an astrologer, guru or therapist, from a spouse or your kids, from doing something or doing nothing.

Just make sure you get one.

Then put all these opinions aside and make the decision your inner astrologer tells you is the best one ... for you.

SUCCESSFUL BUSINESS DECISIONS UNDER PRESSURE!

Over the years some successful friends have given me a few memorable clues as to how they make their key business decisions when they're under pressure and the going's tough. Here are a few examples for you to mull over:

TELEVISION WRITER: "I just get up in the morning, walk out the door and go straight ahead. If I hit a brick wall, I turn left." I thought about this for a while and then asked him, "What if you run into another brick wall." "Turn right," was his sage advise. Eighteen years as a successful writer for a guy who never got past fourth grade English and yet sold his first script to a major series.

FILM SCREENWRITER: "Get into action. If you just sit on your ass, God will just sit there next to you, waiting." This guy's a successful novelist with four feature films to his credit, and before that 200 episodes as a television actor.

TELEVISION & FILM ACTOR: "You run like hell out to left field, and you keep running, then suddenly you wind up in right field. I don't know how you get in right field. But I do know, if you aren't running to left field, you never get to right field." He did seventeen years of bit parts before becoming a superstar.

The Astrology Of Successful Decision-Making

7. THE POWER OF TOTAL COMMITMENT

> **SUCCESS RULE #7.**
> JUST DO IT ... GET INTO ACTION WITH TOTAL COMMITMENT!
> "Staying Power" Means Staying In The Game, No Matter What.
> Don't Quit 5 Minutes Before The Miracle Happens.

Actually, your decision - your commitment, your actions and willingness to hang in there through the rough times - should be the first step in the process, not the last. In fact, it really could be your only step, particularly if you're in harmony with your inner astrologer.

Why? Because if you are *not* passionately committed to *take action,* then all the steps, the techniques and the coaching are just a wasted academic exercise.

Bluntly stated, you must be committed to *yourself* even *before* you identify your target and *before* you're know whether the timing's right.

The key is *your* commitment to *your* decision.

You're making the decision *up front* based on your gut instincts and blind faith. And that is the core of every creative and entrepreneurial venture!

This is what Napoleon Hill calls a *burning desire* and *definiteness of purpose,* coupled with a *positive mental attitude,* or what Anthony Robbins simply calls *passion.* This is what I call the voice of your *inner astrologer.*

YOUR INNER ASTROLOGER IN ACTION ... THE 3 STEPS TO SUCCESS

The message of Hill and Robbins made a very strong impression on me, echoing in my brain while advising a rather aggressive and challenging client. For a number of years I had been using the seven rules of the new Money Astrology Formula as a guide and structure to making business, career and financial decisions.

Then one day a few years ago I was counseling with a transplanted New York City entrepreneur on a career change. At the time, he just had sold a successful retail clothing business and wanted to get into film and television. I remember calling him a *gun-slinging guru* because he acted like a *new age* Elmer Gantry.

"If you didn't have my birth data and all your astrological research, what would you do to help me?" he asked.

It was good question, forcing me to think about what I do with people. After a short pause, my thoughts about a success formula seemed obvious.

What would I do without the astrology?

Here's how I described my thinking process.

What I'd do *without* the astrological data is probably the same thing I'd do with it. After all, if Jung's synchronicity concept is true, you are your own best astrologer. So all we have to do is pry it out of you! And here's how we do it:

ONE. YOUR GOALS: First, I would find out what you really want to do, what are *your goals?* What is that secret dream you have always had since childhood. That special something you say you'll do when you get enough money or enough time ... or maybe not until you get to the next lifetime.

TWO. YOUR OBSTACLES: Next, I'd get you to tell me why you aren't doing what you want to do. Why you aren't going after your own goals. There's probably a damn good reason! I'd also find out if these obstacles are permanent blocks, or just temporary exaggerated fears holding you back, the universe's way of positioning you until the right time.

THREE. YOUR ACTIONS: Finally, I'd give you *permission* to do what you already want to do. Actually, it's much more than mere permission - it's encouragement, motivation, inspiration, coaching, *a push!*

Along with that I'd help you put together an action plan, a budget, timetable, resources, and other essentials, and then tap into your passion for the goal and motivate you into action. *Whatever it takes* to get you out of your rut. I'll do to get you past your fears and into action!

But in the final analysis, you're the one playing the game, calling the plays, and getting roughed up by the competition, I'm just the coach on the sidelines.

> **SUCCESS TIP:** When you know absolutely deep within and are totally committed to your dream, as an echo of the cosmic dream, the power of the universe *will* support your faith. Then the focus shifts from the obstacles to your objectives and you will *feel the fear and just do it anyway! Nothing can stop you.*

In my experience I have found that virtually *everyone has a dream in their life,* some passionate vision that sings loudly deep within their soul ... and fear is their biggest adversary.

They know what they want but they are afraid. "The major weakness of most men is that they recognize the obstacles they must surmount," says Napoleon Hill in his book, *The Master Keys To Riches,* "without recognizing the spiritual power at their command by which those obstacles may be removed at will."

WHEN IT'S TIME TO STOP *THINKING* ... AND GET INTO ACTION!

In my favorite story from *Think & Grow Rich,* Napoleon Hill brings home his central theme that "definiteness of purpose" and a "burning desire" are the starting point for success in life. Mission and passion. Hill illustrates his point with the story of Dr. Frank Gunsaulus, founder of Illinois institute of Technology, a minister with a burning obsession, but no money. His story is powerful:

"One Saturday afternoon I sat in my room thinking of ways and means of raising the money to carry out my plans. For nearly two years, I had been thinking, but I had done nothing but think!

"The time had come for action!

"I made up my mind, then and there, that I would get the necessary million dollars within a week. The main thing of importance was the *decision* to get the money within a specified time, and I want to tell you that the moment I reached a definite decision to get the money within a specific time, a strange feeling of assurance came over me, such as I have never before experienced. Something inside me seemed to say, 'Why didn't you reach that decision a long time ago? The money was waiting for you all the time.' "

> **CAN YOU SEE YOURSELF WITH AN EXTRA $1,000,000?**
> Dr. Gunsaulus was so confident of his decision that he even made a call to the media and announced the topic of his sermon, *"What I Would Do If I Had a Million Dollars,"* which he wrote later that evening. "I could see myself already in possession of the million dollars." Within 24 hours he had the money!

THE POWER OF TOTAL COMMITMENT

The next day, on Sunday morning when Dr. Gunsaulus walked into the pulpit, he discovered that in his haste he had left his notes at home, so "I closed my eyes, and spoke with all my heart and soul of my dreams."

When he finished his sermon he sat down.

"A man slowly arose from his seat, about three rows from the rear, and made his way to the pulpit. I wondered what he was going to do. He came into the pulpit, extended his hand, and said, 'Reverend, I liked your sermon. *I believe you can do everything you said you would,* if you had the million dollars. To prove that I believe you and your sermon, if you come to my office tomorrow morning, I will give you the million dollars. My name is Phillip D. Armour.'"

Now that shows the power of a commitment.

The man had achieved his goal in less than 24 hours ... once his decision was made! The formula for success was simple. No matter what *your* dream, make a decision, building on your "burning desire" or passion, focus yourself with a "definiteness of purpose," then ... *go for it, get into action!*

It's simple, and it works.

TODAY "BURNING DESIRE" MEANS BURNING YOUR BRIDGES ... AND WHAT'S LEFT IS YOUR INNER ASTROLOGER, YOU & THE FORCE.

Although the story has been often told - by Robbins, von Oech and others - Napoleon Hill was probably the first to tell the story in this century, a story illustrating the meaning of *totally committed action*.

A LESSON IN MILITARY STRATEGY

You may recall that when the Spanish explorer Cortez landed at Veracruz in the 16th Century, he burned his ships after unloading his equipment. Then he gave his men a big pep talk, "You can either fight or die," writes the management consultant, Roger von Oech, in his book *A Whack On The Side Of The Head*. "What he did by burning his ships was to eliminate a third alternative, namely turning tail and going back to Spain."

"Sometimes it takes more creativity to get rid of the excuses we put in the way than it does to come up with the idea in the first place. What three factors will make it difficult for you to reach your objective? How can you get rid of your excuses?" *Everyone* **needs these occasional reminders.**

The intensity of this kind of committed action *is* the work of your *inner astrologer*, driven by the cosmic power of The Force. No astrologer *and no one outside of you* can give it to you. It is what Napoleon Hill and Anthony Robbins both called *The Giant Within You.*

Your *inner astrologer* is that *still small voice* the great masters say is guiding us along the road to success in the world of business and finance. It is the inner faith and passion that compelled Robert Prizig, author of *Zen and the Art of Motorcycle Maintenance*, onward in spite of the 134 pre-publication rejections, for a book that's now on many *all-time* best-seller lists.

Focus on your target, *many will try to distract you.*
Know your turning points, *obstacles will deceive you.*
Never rely on the "experts," *in the end you're the only expert.*
Commit to your plan of action, *a mission takes a lot of gruntwork.*
Then burn the escape routes, *force yourself into new solutions.*
In short, just do it. *Be a winner ... just don't quit five minutes before the miracle happens, no matter what.*

SUCCESS IS "THIS THING CALLED YOU"

In the final analysis you must be your own guru, your own hero.
Nobody else can make your decisions.
Only you.
You are the best guide and teacher you will ever have, even though you may, at times, give away your power to others along The Path.
Learn from your experiences.
When the chips are down, it is your decisions alone that will empower your business, your career and your fortune.
This is your life, live it with passion.
For some additional inspiration today, take time to read the spiritual meditations in Ernest Holmes' classic, *This Thing Called You.*
Rediscover the real you.
Create a new you!

PART THREE: APPENDICES

EPILOGUE, RESOURCES & READINGS ON THE NEW MONEY A$TROLOGY

EPILOGUE 2001
A NEW PARADIGM ... A NEW ASTROLOGY!

For the 6,000 years prior to the 20th Century, the *technology* of astrology changed very little.

Today, however, we are experiencing a quantum leap to a new 21st Century astrology which is emerging out of the intense stress and unpredictable chaos of the world-wide paradigm shift of the late 20th Century.

As a result, in less than a century, astrology has advanced far more than it had in the prior 6,000 years!

In this new reality, extreme stress, chaos and instability are essential elements in this process of transformation. Biologists call this sudden creative leap, a *punctuated equilibrium*. Physicists refer to Bell's theorem. Chemists refer to this change as the Zhabotinskii reaction and the theory of *dissipative structures.*

Regardless of who's looking at the phenomenon, scientists agree, *something new* is suddenly born out of the chaotic processes of transformation, like the Phoenix arising from the ashes.

The process can take many forms; super-novas and political revolutions, post-traumatic stress syndrome and paranormal phenomena, enlightenment and psychotic splits, mutant gene formations and spiritual rebirths.

FUTURE SUCCESS: COSMIC CONTROLS OR CREATIVE CHAOS?

A decade ago, The astronomer, Carl Sagan, taught us that "*Cosmos* is a Greek word for order in the Universe ... the opposite of *Chaos*." Sagan emphasized that *order* should have a higher value for us as we are emerge "from the Chaos of the Big Bang to the Cosmos ..." Today, you should be aware that the paradigm shift is reversing these "scientific" values.

"For the last 30 years, most of us have thought we were in the information age. Research done by the Nomura Research Institute, Japan's leading think tank, says forget it;" according to Tom Peters, author of *Liberation Management, In Search of Excellence* and *Thriving on Chaos,* "the information age is just about behind us. Now we are headed for a new era of 'creation intensification,' or the age of brainware."

In a *Working Women* magazine article "Thriving in Chaos," Peters goes on to say, "Corporate America is literally falling apart," and the new "No. 1 role of tomorrow's senior executive: screw things up. The definition of success now is experiment, experiment, experiment." Order, control, logic and rationality are being replaced, or at least challenged, by chaos, creativity, relativity, artificial intelligence, fuzzy logic, virtual reality and management by muddling around.

If you expect to be one of tomorrow's winners, you cannot ignore Tom Peters' warnings of a future that's already here, "Take all your cherished assumptions. Don't modify them one bit. Throw them out." Including all your prior beliefs about astrology. *Now is the time for you to experiment, later may be too late!*

The greater the instability, the greater potential for a major leap forward ... *or destruction.* As Nietzsche once said, "that which does not destroy us will set us free." This freedom releases the inherent power of the new order.

The "new species arises suddenly ... it does not evolve gradually by the steady change of its ancestors, but all at once and fully formed," and there are no *missing links,* according to Stephen Jay Gould, the Harvard University biologist responsible for the theory of *punctuated equilibrium* discussed in Ferguson's *Aquarian Conspiracy. A new being emerges full-blown.*

Today you are witnessing a parallel phenomenon in astrology, a paradigm shift, a practical revolution, a qualitative transformation. The main causes are:

- the **new computer technology**, which has made possible advances in both the astronomy of space travel and the new astrology, and
- the **leadership of a few historical giants**, such as Morgan, Jung, Gann, Gauquelin and Williams.

This transformation of modern astrology has generated a strong conservative backlash, however, with a tendency to reject new ideas. And in order to protect against potential negative reactions, individual clients typically keep their visits to astrologers confidential, much as they keep confidential their meetings with their physicians, attorneys and tax accountants.

This tendency toward *secrecy* has kept astrology out of the limelight and operating discreetly behind the scenes. It has also kept the real progress of the emerging new 21st Century astrology under wraps and away from a skeptical and sensationalistic press that thrives on the old paradigm. The public and the press are still judging astrology largely from the perspective of the old paradigm, and only faintly aware of an emerging new order. Many astrologers are also unaware of the dramatic changes around them.

And yet, while it is possible that the public and the press will not fully perceive or appreciate this new astrology until we arrive at the 21st Century, its principle elements are clearly discernable as we have outlined in this book. In fact, a recent *Business Week* article even called this change in public acceptance "the dawning of the age of financial astrology," suggesting that *tomorrow has already arrived ... ahead of schedule!*

THE NEW 21st CENTURY ASTROLOGER IS HERE, NOW, TODAY!

The new Money A$trology is a strong expression of this emerging new order for the 21st Century. It recognizes the collective input of finance, psychology, science, mythology and creative genius, while defining a *unified formula* that structures a decision-making process using astrology, as we have seen in the seven rules of this new Money A$trology.

Within this broad framework we will see emerge a whole new set of astrologer-specialists. *Hyphenate-astrologers* as I call them, highly-skilled in a traditional profession - such as stock brokerage, business management, computer technology, psychotherapy, medicine, and others - while actively using astrology as an *"edge" to achieve peak performance* in their work. If you look around, you will see the signs of this new order all around us today.

My adventure into astrology began with several wonderful opportunities:

. the mythic "Journey of The Hero" Joseph Campbell introduced into my life while I was working in the Wall Street investment banking House of Morgan,

. my first taste of Jungian psychology from Francesca, an Italian ballerina and my alter ego, who totally turned on my creative juices,

. Marilyn Ferguson, whose ground-breaking research on the *Aquarian Conspiracy* inspired me to a doctorate on the processes of transformation, chaos, crisis and creativity, and

. Sydney Omarr and a psychic friend of his who peaked my curiosity about the para-normal by insisting that H.G. Wells reincarnated as this arch-skeptic.

My vision of the emerging new astrology of the 21st century was forged out of these and many other powerful experiences that went into *the making of this astrologer* over the last fifty years. This adventure in professional and personal transformation will continue well into the 21st Century, as we all participate in the larger, dynamic revolution created by the paradigm shift impacting every segment of our planet and civilization. *Be there!*

APPENDIX ONE:
DIRECTORY of RESOURCES FOR THE EMERGING NEW ASTROLOGY

COMPUTER SOFTWARE & BOOK PUBLISHERS & SUPPLIERS
AIR Software, West Hartford, CT (203) 232-6521
American Federation of Astrologers, Tempe, AZ (602) 838-1751
Astrocalc British Astrological Software, U.K. 0442-251809
Astro Communications Services, San Diego (800) 888-9983
Astrolabe, Inc., Brewster, MA (800) 843-6682
Astrology Services International, New York City (212) 947-3702
Cosmic Patterns, Gainesville, FL (904) 373-1504
Foundation for the Study of Cycles, Wayne, PA (215) 995-2120
Llewellyn Publications, St. Paul, MN (800) 843-6666
Matrix Software, Inc., Big Rapids, MI (800) 752-6387
MicroCycles, Los Angeles, CA (800) 829-2537
Trader's World Catalogue, Springfield, MO (800) 288-4266

BOOKS ON MONEY A$TROLOGY & CYCLES RESEARCH
Berg, *The Astro Method*
Bradley, *Stock Market Prediction*
Dewey & Mandino, *Cycles: Mysterious Forces That Trigger Events*
Dewey & Dakin, *Cycles: The Science of Prediction*
Gann, *The Magic Word; New Stock Trend Selector: 45 Years in Wall Street*
Jensen, *Astro-Cycles & Speculative Markets*
Koval, *Money & Time*
McEver, *Financial Astrology for The 1990's*
McWhirter, *Astrology & Stock Market Forecasting*
Merriman, *The Gold Book: GeoCosmic Correlations To Gold Price Cycles*
Pesavento, *Astro-Cycles - A Trader's Viewpoint*
Williams, *Astro-Economics; Financial Astrology*

NEWSLETTERS & PERIODICALS ON MONEY A$TROLOGY
Berg, *Whole Earth Forecaster* (402) 558-2300
Bost, *Financial Cycles* (800) 995-2068
Crawford, *Crawford Perspectives* (212) 628-1156
Eliades, *StockMarket Cycles* (707) 579-8444
Foundation for the Study of Cycles, *Cycles Magazine* (215) 995-2120
Hardy, *Economic Forecasts, Moon Sign Book* (800) 843-6666
Jacobs, *The Trader's World* (417) 882-9697
Long, *Traders Astrological Almanac; GRF Journal* (305) 566-2636
Meridian, *Cycles Research* (Abu Dhabi) 9712-786402
Merriman, *MMA Cycles Report* (313) 626-3034
Mull, *The Astro-Investor* (317) 357-6855
Pesavento, *Astro-Cycles* (805) 773-0412
Sexton, *Harmonic Research* (212) 484-2065
Winski, *Astro-Trend* (813) 261-7261

CONFERENCES ON MONEY A$TROLOGY
Long, *Global Research Forum* (305) 566-2636
Morris, *Conference for Astro-Economics* (708) 636-3858
Mull, *Astro-Timing Techniques for Traders & Investors* (317) 357-6855
Weingarten, *Astrology & Stock Market Forecasting* (212) 947-3540

NATAL ASTROLOGY, CAREERS & PERSONAL POWER
Arroyo, *Relationships & Life Cycles; Astrology, Psychology & The Four Elements*
Binder, *Planets in Work: A Complete Guide to Vocational Astrology*
Bloch & George, *Astrology For Yourself*
March & McEvers, *The Only Way To Learn Astrology*
Pottenger, *Complete Horoscope Interpretation*
Rathgeb, *Success Signs*

PERSONAL FORECASTING WITH ASTRO-CYCLES
Arroyo, *Relationships & Life Cycles*
Forrest, *The Inner Sky; The Changing Sky*
Gauquelin, *Cosmic Clocks; Written In The Stars; The Scientific Basis of Astrology*
Hand, *Planets in Transits*
Lewis, *Astro*Carto*Graphy*
Martin, *Astrocycles*
Townley, *Astrological Life Cycles*
West, *The Case For Astrology*

FUTURISM & FUTURE FORECASTING
Capra, *The Tao of Physics; The Turning Point*
Ferguson, *The Aquarian Conspiracy*
Gleick, *Chaos, Making A New Science*
Kuhn, *The Structure of Scientific Revolutions*
Naisbett & Aburdene, *Megatrends for Women; Megatrends 2000*
Peters, *In Search of Excellence; Liberation Management; Thriving on Chaos*
Popcorn, *The Popcorn Report*
Ray, *The New Paradigm in Business*
Russell, *The Global Brain*
Schaef, *Beyond Therapy, Beyond Science*
Toffler, *The Third Wave; Future Shock; The Power Shift*

BUSINESS & PERSONAL MOTIVATION
Brown, *Live Your Dreams*
Covey, *The 7 Habits of Highly Effective People; Principle-Centered Leadership*
Fisher, *The Instant Millionaire*
Hill & Stone, *Success Through Positive Mental Attitude*
Hill, *Think & Grow Rich; You Can Work Your Own Miracles*
Holmes, *This Thing Called You*
Hawken, *Growing A Business*
Leonard, *Mastery*
Peck, *The Road Less Travelled*
Robbins, *Awaken The Giant Within*
von Oech, *A Kick In The Seat Of The Pants*
Waitley, *The Psychology of Winning*

MARKET & INVESTMENT STRATEGIES
Dreman, *Psychology & the Stock Market; New Contrarian Investment Strategy*
Lynch, *One Up On Wall Street; Beating The Street*
Malkiel, *A Random Walk Down Wall Street*

CAREER PLANNING & PERSONALITY TESTING
Kroeger & Thuesen, *Type Talk; Type Talk at Work*
Keirsey & Bates, *Please Understand Me*
Perkins-Reed, *When 9-to-5 Isn't Enough*
Sinetar, *Do What You Love & The Money Will Follow*
Tieger, *Do What You Are*

APPENDIX 1: RESOURCES & READINGS

STRESS MANAGEMENT & MEDITATION
Borysenko, *Fire In The Soul*
Charlesworth, *Stress Management*
Groves, *Meditation For Busy People*
Huang, *T'ai Chi; Embrace Tiger, Return To Mountain*
LeSaun, *The Art Of Meditation*
Mindell, *Working With Yourself Alone*
Rajneesh, *The Goose is Out; The Orange Book; The Search; Meditation*
Selye, *The Stress of Life*

LIFE-CRISIS MANAGEMENT
Bragdon, *The Call of Spiritual Emergency*
Bridges, *Transitions*
Colgrove, *How To Survive The Loss of A Love*
Sheehy, *Passages; Pathfinders*
Slaikeu, *The Phoenix Factor*
Smith, *Powers of Mind*

JUNGIAN PSYCHOLOGY & MYTHOLOGY
Campbell, *The Masks of God; Hero of A 1000 Faces; The Power of Myth*
Edinger, *Ego & Archetype*
Feinstein, *Personal Mythology*
Jacobi, *The Way of Individuation*
Jung, *Analytical Psychology; Man & His Symbols; Synchronicity*
Kopp, *Mirror, Mask & Shadow; If You Meet The Buddha On The Road, Kill Him*
Moore, *Care of The Soul*
Pearson, *Awakening The Heros Within; Six Archetypes To Live By*

ZEN & THE TAO
Beetcher, *Beyond Success and Failure*
Fields, *Chop Wood, Carry Water*
Goodspeed, *The Tao Jones Averages*
Herrigel, *Zen and the Art of Archery*
Heider, *The Tao of Leadership*
Hoff, *The Tao of Pooh*
Hyams, *Zen & The Martial Arts*
Musashi, *The Book of Five Rings*
Pirzig, *Zen & The Art of Motorcycle Maintenance*
Watts, *The Spirit of Zen; The Way of Zen; The Wisdom of Insecurity*
Zukav, *The Dancing Wu Li Masters*

THE MASCULINE JOURNEY
Farrell, *Why Men Are The Way They Are; The Myth of Male Power*
Goldberg, *The Hazards of Being Male*
Gould, *Transformations*
Keen, *Fire In The Belly*
Levinson, *Seasons of a Man's Life*
Mayer, *The Male Midlife Crisis*

THE FEMININE JOURNEY
Andrews, *Crystal Woman; Jaguar Woman; Star Woman*
Leonard, *Meeting The Mad Woman*
Murdock, *The Heroine's Journey*
Norwood, *Women Who Love Too Much*
Pinkola Estes, *Women Who Run With The Wolves*
Schaef, *A Nation of Addicts; Woman's Reality*

> **SUCCESS TIP: PICKING THE BEST ASTROLOGER FOR YOU**
> You know that selecting the right consultants of any kind is a key to success in any business, and often a very risky decision. Therefore, with the many new sub-specialties emerging in the new astrology, you need to be aware of these distinctions discussed here, before you pick an astrological advisor.
> For example, you may not want a financial astrologer for general career counseling. You also may not want a financial astrologer specializing in the commodities markets to help you make a decision about choosing new business partners. Also see the appendices for a checklist on selecting astrologers.
> Henry Weingarten, investment advisor to The Astrologer's Fund notes that astrology can be a valuable tool in helping investors develop their *investment style* and select an appropriate *market niche*. Armed with this quasi-psychological, astrological information you can better select the right astrological advisor for you, as well as avoid certain financial securities.
> In addition, Weingarten encourages *professionalism*. While I suggest that you rely on your *inner astrologer* in the absence of reliable alternatives, unless you are professional trained - especially in the stock market - you may be wise to work with a mentor at first, rather than totally *fly blind* on your gut instincts.

APPENDIX TWO
HOW TO PICK THE "RIGHT" ASTROLOGER
Six Questions You Should Ask

Writing in *Smart Money*, sports super-agent Mark McCormack, the author of *What They Don't Teach You In Harvard*, reveals his investment strategy, "Bet on the jockey, not the horse." In our context that means your choice of an astrologer will be more important than their brand of astrology.

Unfortunately, you have a 65%+ chance of picking the *wrong* astrologer. If you do, you're likely to get *information that's either useless, or worse yet, misleading*. That could be a disaster - if you're making a decision to switch careers, invest in a new project, start a new business, or market a new product.

Still, you need advice. You're at a crossroads. Maybe you just want a "second opinion" ... someone other than your therapist, attorney, guru, or mate, because you have nagging doubts about your direction and your decisions at this key turning point.

So how can you *improve* your odds of picking the right astrologer?

Start by asking these six key questions, *before you pick one:*

QUESTION #1: "ANY TRAINING IN COUNSELING & PSYCHOLOGY?"

First of all, you need an astrologer who has a solid foundation in the science of psychology, especially with relationship issues. Many astrologers are still in the Dark Ages.

For example, a few years ago, an astrologer with over 50 years of experience was questioning me about the theories of Ptolemy, an ancient astrologer of the second century A.D. In turn, I asked her if she ever heard of the "DSM-3" (*Diagnostic & Statistical Manual of Mental Disorders,* published by the American Psychiatric Association).

No, she hadn't. Yet this book is a basic Bible for all psychologists, therapists and many other mental health counselors. It's unfortunate that astrologers are not at least aware of this and other such key works. How else can they grasp the issues underlying their clients' relationships?

The psychologist, Dr. Carl Jung, was a master astrologer. Astrological charts were a regular part of his preliminary diagnoses. In one of his studies, he observed 97% accuracy using astrology as a predictive tool.

Jung's theory of "synchronicity" is based on the connection between our internal human DNA/genes and the external electromagnetic of interplanetary motion. Jung concluded that, "astrology represents the summation of all psychological knowledge of antiquity." Today's astrologers *must* study *both*.

Fortunately, Jung's work has encouraged many psychologists and healthcare professionals to use astrology as a diagnostic tool. Similarly, several authors of today's basic texts on modern astrology, including Stephen Arroyo and Robert Hand, were originally trained in psychology. As a result, they are raising the level of awareness, if not the expertise, of their fellow astrologers. Is your's one of them?

Before picking an astrologer, you should find out about their understanding of and training in psychology, keeping in mind that this skill must focus on *mass* psychology - rather than *individual* psychology - if your main interests are astro-economics, stock market trading and Money Astrology.

QUESTION #2: "WHAT'S YOUR EXPERIENCE IN THE BUSINESS WORLD?"

In addition to asking this astrologer with 50 years experience about the DSM3 manual used by psychologists, I also asked her if she'd ever used a *discounted cashflow analysis (DCF)* when advising a client on a business project?" Another blank stare. I didn't have the guts to ask her about Gann's theories.

Discounting cashflow is a way for investors to adjust for the value of money received in the future. I was first exposed to it back in the Sixties, when I developed some computer software programs for real estate investment analysis while was working for a large architectural-engineering firm. Discounting cashflow to present value is basic in any business forecasting, yet this astrologer had never heard of it.

You need an astrologer with *practical* experience working in a business or world. Making money, making decisions, making mistakes and balancing a business with personal relationships. And succeeding in the process. Some grounding in the real world of business is essential.

Astrology is often as important in big business and financial decisions as economics and statistics. In the last century, for example, many successful business and financial leaders have been using astrology to predict the future - stock market trends, new business starts, career decisions, contract signings, real estate decisions. J. P. Morgan said, "millionaires don't hire astrologers, billionaires do!" His astrologer once wrote that she was also advising three successive presidents of the New York Stock Exchange. And the technical analysis methods commonly used today by most Wall Street market analysts originated with an astrologer-mathematician, W. D. Gann, who made $50 million with his trading methods.

If you're looking for advice on your career, business, finances, investments, real estate or similar decisions, you need an astrologer who has some experience in these matters. Otherwise, you may get someone with a limited perspective, who knows the mathematics of calculating charts and transits, and merely dresses it up in some entertaining New Age jargon!

Don't compromise. Ask the tough questions about your astrologer's business experience, *before picking one.*

QUESTION #3: "IS YOUR ASTROLOGY GROUNDED IN SCIENCE?"

Carl Jung once complained that astrology lacked a scientific basis, that it had not been "tested." Michel Gauquelin picked up the challenge, and for decades he conducted extensive scientific correlation studies of the birth data of 500,000 successful leaders in business, sports, politics, medicine, the military and sciences. Gauquelin's research - and his emphasis on a scientific approach - has filtered into the teachings and writings of several astrologers/career consultants. Many astrologers are still relying primarily on their unsupported "psychic powers," with minimum scientific grounding. Some are even *against* science, or anything that *restricts* their intuitive powers or creativity.

Where does your astrologer stand? Question your astrologer on their use of the scientific method.

QUESTION #4: "WHAT KIND OF RESULTS ARE YOU GETTING?"

This question is a double-edged sword ... to the astrologer *before* you hire them and to yourself *after* you hire an astrologer.

Most of the time, selecting an astrologer is risky. So, the bottom-line is ... are you getting good results? Results are really all that counts in any business. If you are getting solid advice on a repeat basis, stick with your astrologer! In the

APPENDIX 2: PICK THE RIGHT ASTROLOGER

end, in spite of all my warnings, it doesn't matter *where* the astrologer gets their information, if it's actually working for you!

But, just maybe the astrologer is *only reading your mind, that is, picking up your brain waves and merely reflecting back your own wishful thinking,* further hypnotizing you with your own preconceptions. Maybe their brand of astrology is just window-dressing, to create an illusion of a special link to "the other side."

They may also be a charlatan, making it all up as they go along, "reading" your body language for clues of what you want to hear. Maybe they're just a skillful con artist, guessing, conjuring a future that, statistically, anyone like you might dream of! You really don't know, until it may be too late. Test them! And accelerate *your* paradigm shift.

Remember, the results come only *after* you work with your astrologer. *Beforehand, ask questions, ask lots of questions!*

QUESTION #5: "WHERE DOES 'FREE-WILL' FIT INTO YOUR WORK?"

Many astrologers actually believe that astrological "predictions" are *predetermined* forecasts of the future. Nonsense, they're no different than a AAA roadmap. You *always* have the freedom to change your "destiny" and take another road! In fact, if Jung's principle of synchronicity means anything, *you are your own best astrologer,* because of the link between your genes and the planets. You choose to respond or not to the electromagnetic energies of the universe. *Trust your own instincts!*

Astrological consultations should be an interactive, creative process, with the astrologer *merely helping the client discover their own solutions.* One client, a skeptical banker, was at a critical turning point in his career. While he didn't believe in astrology, he was hoping that our sessions would trigger new solutions, one's he had missed. He was in a rut, like many left-brained businessmen. He wanted a creative *whack on the side of the head,* and got it!

Find out how rigid your astrologer is about their "predictions."

QUESTION #6: "HOW DID YOUR 'SPIRITUAL' BELIEFS DEVELOP?"

Luckily, my first astrology lesson came from Joseph Campbell, the great scholar on mythology. Like Michel Gauquelin, he was influenced by the ideas and research of Carl Jung. What a gift! Campbell magically linked astrology to Jungian psychology, mythic archetypes, Zen Buddhism, Taoism, Hopi shamanism, medieval Christian mysticism and The Tarot. Campbell awakened a new spirit in my life.

Over the years, my *spiritual* processes have also been heavily influenced by the 12-Step Programs and Science of Mind, by the works of Alan Watts, Arnie Mindell, Marilyn Ferguson, John Bradshaw and Goethe, by the United States Marine Corps, est and the Esalen Institute, by Indiana Jones, Star Trek and Close Encounters of The Third Kind, by J. P. Morgan, Mother Teresa and my Uncle Mickey, the mailman, by a belief in a loving Higher Power that I really don't understand, because like Jacob, I often find myself *wrestling with God,* asking why life is unfair, why bad things happen to good people. My values are solid, but they are not rigidly locked into one organized religious system.

In the end I always seem to come back fighting to *be all that I can be,* striving to inspire myself and those around me reach our highest potentials, to be *this thing called you* as Ernest Holmes would say, to *individuate* as Jung described it, to become *enlightened* in the Zen tradition, to live a full life, to come at life with a Positive Mental Attitude!

Before hiring *your* astrologer, question them about their "spiritual" beliefs.

APPENDIX THREE
A PLAN OF ACTION WHEN ALL ELSE FAILS
"THE CRISIS SURVIVAL KIT"

WAKE-UP CALLS, TURNING POINTS, MIRACLES & NEW BEGINNINGS

So you just had one of life's many "wake-up calls?"
Congratulations!
A new business venture, career or promotion. A new romance. A marriage. A new baby. A midlife transition. Health problems. The loss of a loved one, or a job. Or maybe you're ready to give up an addiction and start a new life.

Every journey begins with a wake-up call. Always unique, often sudden and unexpected.

An exciting opportunity, a challenge, a crisis. This one can be different, a new beginning. A chance to get out of the old ruts, break old habits, leave behind your addictions. A chance to start living your dreams.

Wake-up. This is a turning point. Be thankful for the gift.

A WINNING FORMULA: 10 KEYS TO TOTAL SUCCESS IN A CRISIS

Key #1: MAKE A DECISION ... And Say "Yes" To Success!

First, *you* must make a decision. Otherwise you're powerless, at the mercy of external events and other people controlling your life.

Change is an "inside job." The wake-up call is an opportunity to transform who you are. Many ignore it, cling to the status quo, and sink deeper into their problems.

You must make a decision. Or it will be made for you.

Hopefully, the promise of an exciting, new future is so powerful you are compelled to "go for it." And with luck, the pain of the old ways is so intolerable, you willingly accept new directions.

Make the decision. Say "yes" to success!

Decisions give you power and set you free. Decisions are the first key to turning dreams into reality. Put the formula into action. It works!

Key #2: THE TRANSITION - Interrupt Old Behaviors, Anchor New Ones.

During the transition period you are confronted with the mixed blessing of endings and new beginnings. Old habits die hard. New ones are often painfully frustrating. Resistance is a natural part of the process.

In the crucial early stages of a major change you take "contrary actions," resisting old beliefs, deprogramming limitations. While affirming and reinforcing the new reality, you may even have to "fake it 'til you make it." You are an alien on the road less travelled. In this aloneness, you discover a new source of power. You may be tested often. Obstacles, adversities and problems are common. Winning demands persistence. You will need guides, mentors and a loving support system to cheer you on.

Slowly you will discover the joy of living a new way. New behaviors bring new pleasures, reinforcing your decision. Eventually, the new way becomes a part of you, and it becomes the *only* way.

APPENDIX 3: CRISIS SURVIVAL KIT

YOU ARE A WHOLE SYSTEM: FAMILY, FITNESS, FINANCES, FAITH & FUN.
Total success demands a balanced mixture of all five major areas of your life; family, fitness, finances, faith and fun. Each one must be a top priority, of equal status, guiding you as a matter of principle:

Key #3: FAMILY - Success in All Your Relationships, Love & Work.
Relationships are the cornerstone of a successful life. We need healthy family bonds, with our mates, children, parents and other relatives. With our extended families outside the home, our friends and social ties. And with the network of relationships that makeup our daily business contacts. Success means making relationships a priority, not an afterthought. Success means giving more than you receive, while surrounding yourself with a total "win/win" support system. Successful relationships make life worth living.

Key #4: FITNESS - Success With Your Body, Nutrition & Health.
A sound body is another essential element in the total success formula. The body is the physical glue binding everything else - relationships, career, emotions and spirit. When you say yes to success, you commit to creating a strong, healthy body. This means a regular program of exercise, for strength and endurance. You commit to control the "fuel" you put in your body, what you eat and how much. You watch what you breath, avoiding nicotine and the excessive use of drugs and alcohol. Stress is managed as a positive force. You build a "body machine" with the energy and power ready for peak performance. You build a new you.

Key #5: FINANCES - Success With Your Career, Business & Money.
The single most important key to your financial success and prosperity is the ability to "add value" to the lives of other people. Whatever your services, products, business or profession, if you consistently help others improve the quality of their lives, you will be rewarded. What goes around comes around. Help others gain wealth and you will become wealthy. Be a winner. Think smart. Act with integrity. Develop a specialized niche. Expand your skills. Leverage your talents. And always deliver more than you promised. Help others achieve "total success," and you will too.

Key #6: FAITH - Success With Your Higher Power & Your-Self.
Napoleon Hill's classic, *Think and Grow Rich,* is the most "bottom-line" science of success ever developed. Yet Hill discovered that *every one* of the five hundred leaders of industry and finance he studied believed they were guided by "unseen guides;" spiritual powers, universal intelligence, inner wisdom, the other self or God. These leaders instinctively know what God's will is for them and have a confident faith in this inexhaustible source of power. Prayer and meditation enhance their competitive spirit. The leader acts with integrity, self-esteem, confidence and a strong need to serve the highest public good. For these men and women, "awaken the giant within" means being all you can be! This unshakeable faith leads to total success!

Key #7: FUN - Success in Creating A Balanced Life.
"Having it all" must include laughter, pleasure, recreation and peace of mind. Without balance, the road to success will be filled with stress potholes, while Superwoman and the Ironman slowly burnout. Success then becomes a hollow victory. Balance means a diverse mixture of all elements of the total success formula. Everything is included, creating a full life. Learning, lovemaking and legislating. Dancing, dining and deal-making. Step aerobics, step kids and

12 steps. Voting and vacations. Time schedules, time zones and time outs. Municipal bonds, maternal bonds and meditation. Power struggles, higher powers and personal power. Balance. You leave nothing out. Because the whole *is* greater than the sum of the parts.

THE SUCCESS FORMULA AT WORK: "SOLUTIONS-IN-ACTION!"

Key #8: FOCUS ON YOUR GOALS: Goals, Commitments, Plans & Priorities

Once you decide and say yes to success, develop a total game-plan, one that sharply defines your goals and vision, locking on specific targets and specific time-tables, in all areas of your life! Start with a statement of your life's mission, along with affirmations that clearly state your commitment to total success. Develop a strategic plan setting priorities for long-term and near-term targets, and criteria to periodically check your progress. Put it all in writing. Stay totally committed to achieving your mission. And remember, it's easier to set goals than it is to stick by them with integrity.

Key #9: ACTION, ACTION & MORE ACTION!

Once you set your plans and priorities, get into action. Immediately. Start by doing something, anything, to advance you toward your goals. Just do it. And continue taking action on a daily basis. Massive action. Review your priorities often, staying focused on your targets, doing first things first. Total success demands sustained action, often against overwhelming odds. When the going gets tough, the tough keep going. Get your solutions-in-action!

Key #10: COMMITMENT + TENACITY + PERSISTENCE + FLEXIBILITY.

The final key to success requires a special wisdom to know the difference between rigid determination and the flexibility to make necessary changes as your actions continually feedback new information. While "don't give up five minutes before the miracle happens" is a great battle-cry in the face of adversity, in reality you will be forced to make frequent "course corrections" on the way to your target. Yes, you must be persistent. And yes, you must remain flexible. Experience will give you the wisdom to know the difference ... as long as you stay in the action, focused on your goals.

THE ULTIMATE CHALLENGE

Bonus Key #11: LIVING YOUR DREAM, LIVING THE CALL TO GREATNESS.

The ultimate challenge of this formula is to answer your wake-up call, take charge of your life and start living your dreams. Every journey of personal transformation begins with one of these "calls to greatness." You can become a miracle in progress, on the path to self-mastery. Accept the gift you have been given, set your goals high, get into action and discover total success ... start living your dreams, today!

APPENDIX 4: BASIC TOOLS FOR ASTROLOGY

THE BASIC TOOLS FOR ASTROLOGICAL ANALYSIS

The following five tables summarize the basic concepts and techniques discussed in the chapters on the *Seven Basic Rules for Successful Decision-Making*. Our intention is not to make you an expert astrologer, just to get you generally familiar with this analytical process so that you can ask intelligent questions of your astrological consultants.

As we have said several times, this particular kind of astrological analysis is used for *personal* astrology where the focus is on an *individual* person, *individual* psychology and an *individual's* decision-making, rather than *mass* psychology.

Please keep in mind that *even if* you think you are interested *only* in *mass psychology* and the behavior of the financial markets, this information can still be important to you in helping you understand your personality traits, career choices and style of decision-making ... including your method of trading, your risk-taking level and your choice of investments. For more on mass psychology and trading, you should especially review Rule #3 above.

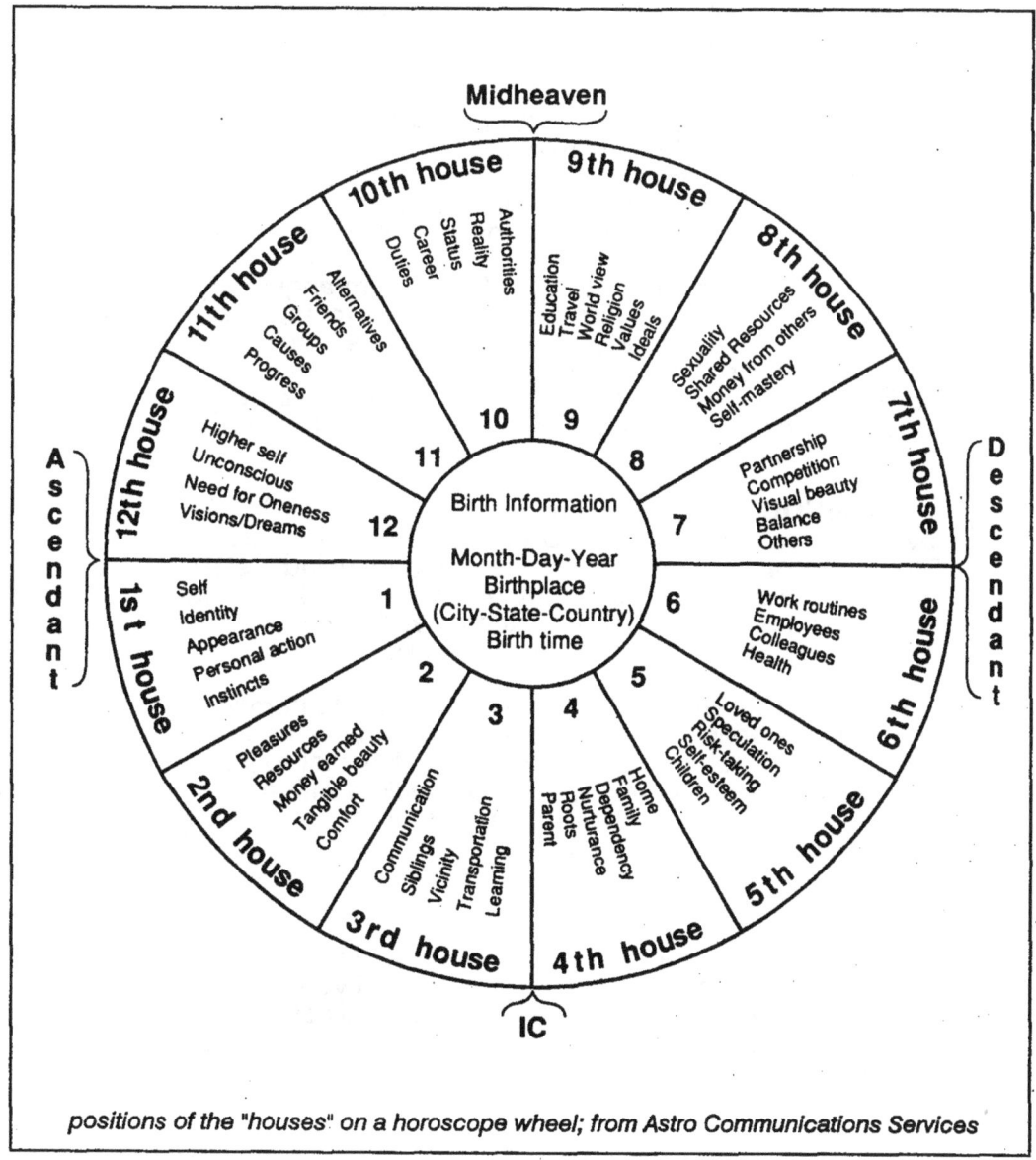

positions of the "houses" on a horoscope wheel; from Astro Communications Services

A "MINI-CRASH COURSE" in Personal Astrology

PLANETS: Our solar system has 10 major planets, including the Sun at the center and the Moon, which is actually a satellite. The others are Mercury, Venus, Mars, Jupiter, Saturn, Uranus, Neptune and Pluto. These planets follow elliptical paths around the Sun within a rather narrow band that is divided into the 12 signs.

SIGNS: The ancient astronomer-astrologers divided the zodiac into 12 convenient sectors of 30 degrees each. The planets travel at different speeds through each of these 12 divisions of the sky. The spring equinox starts the procession with the first sign, Aries, and the others follow in turn, Taurus, Gemini, Cancer, Leo, Virgo, Libra, Scorpio, Sagittarius, Capricorn, Aquarius and Pisces. See the Zip-Codes.

HOUSES: The Earth takes 24 hours to rotate on it's axis making it appear as if all the stars or planets travel through the zodiac in one day. Thus, astrologers created the 12 houses to reflect this daily movement. The houses begin at the Ascendant, which is the Rising Sign on the horizon at the moment of birth. See example on page 113.

ASPECTS: At any moment the planets form angles with one and other. However, astrologers give more importance to certain angles, called aspects. The aspects intensify the energies between the two planets, creating *opportunities* and *challenges*. The main ones are the *Conjunct* (0 degrees), *Sextile* (60 degrees), *Square* (90 degrees), *Trine* (120 degrees) and the *Opposition* (180 degrees).

STAND-OUTS: The birth charts of most individuals that have some *out-standing* astrological features. They are different in combination for each person and include, stellia or several planets close to one another, structural aspects such as grand trines and T-squares, patterns and other features. All these add to the power of the personality.

THE WHOLE PICTURE: There are an infinite number of combinations between the planets, signs, houses and aspects, which reflects each person's uniqueness. In order to interpret your data, get a computer report and check in with an astrologer who is also active in business or the professions, and use March and McEver's *The Only Way to Learn Astrology*, or Bloch & George's *Astrology For Yourself* workbook, if you want more basic background.

TRANSITS: The transits are the dynamic angles made between the current ever-moving planets and your natal planets. These transits are much like the natal aspects, which are static angles determined at the moment of birth. Future transits can be predicted, and therefore are used to forecast likely events and states of mind in the future.

APPENDIX 4: BASIC ASTROLOGY

AN ASTROLOGICAL PROFILE ANALYSIS
Using the 6 "Out-Standing" Power Centers

Here's a summary of what your astrologer might do when they're under time pressure in preparing for an astrological consultation; these are the *out-standing* things to look for:

1. THE "POWER ZONES:" the planets in Dr. Gauquelin's Power Zones, or they are making aspects to the Midheaven and Ascendant. See Gauquelin, *Written in the Stars*, and Binder, *Planets in Work* for comments on planets in these sectors. March and McEvers, *The Only Way to Learn Astrology*, volume II has excellent interpretations for the aspects.

2. ENTREPRENEUR'S "SUCCESS PROFILE:" see which of the elements are dominant then check the following tables, "10 Personality Profiles," noting any back-up interpretations in Arroyo, *Astrology, Psychology and The Four Elements*, and Pottenger, *Complete Horoscope Interpretation*. Note any missing elements and see Arroyo's comments.

3. YOUR "SUCCESS SIGNS:" using Rathgeb's book, *Success Signs*, Arroyo's *Four Elements*, or one of the other resources, check the career and personality interpretations for the Sun, Moon, Ascendant and Midheaven.

4. PLANETS IN "THE HOUSES:" interpret the meaning of each of the planets in their natal houses, checking signs and aspects of the key ones, especially those standing-out for other reasons, such as being part of a T-Square, Grand Trine or Stellia. Use March and McEvers, volume I.

5. THE CHART'S "PATTERN:" visually inspect the chart for any overall patterns that are definable. See Binder's *Planets in Work* or Gauquelin's *Written in The Stars* for examples.

6. UNUSUAL "STAND-OUTS:" next, run a quick visual diagnostic and identify any unusual stuff - stellia, grand trines, T-squares, interceptions, and patterns - checking volume II of March and McEvers for comments.

NOW, PUT IT ALL TOGETHER: now you've got all the facts, so use your own intuition about the personality you have been examining like a doctor. Your judgment is probably as good as the next guy's at this point, so trust the message you get from your *inner astrologer!*

FINALLY, CHECK THE TRANSIT & YOUR FUTURE: Now, what's going on today, and tomorrow! After looking at the natal chart, check the transits. Look at the house transits first, especially which houses Jupiter and Saturn are transiting. See, Arroyo, *Relationship and Life Cycles* and Townley, *Astrological Life Cycles*. Then look at this year's upcoming planet-to-planet transits for Jupiter, Saturn, Uranus, Neptune and Pluto. Hand's *Planets in Transit* is an excellent guide for both the planet-to-planet and the house transits.

THE 10 PERSONALITY PROFILES for BUSINESS SUCCESS.
Basic Styles of Decision-Making with
Your Money, Business, Careers & Investments
THE 4 BASIC PERSONALITY TYPES

These 4 Profiles are Based on the 4 Basic "Elements" and Exist When You Have One Element Dominant:

#1. FIRE POWER. "THE DYNAMO"
An Inspiring, Freedom-Loving Hero.
Fire is energetic and exciting, spontaneous and spirited, dynamic and dramatic, confident and creative, they *know* by intuition, gut reactions and the seat-of-the-pants, optimistic, they have great faith in life and themselves. They are alive, coaching, motivating, leading, searching, traveling, seeking.
- **Aries**: initiator, motivator, cheerleader
- **Leo**: coach, creative brainstormer, dramatic leader
- **Sagittarius**: adventurer, explorer, philosopher

#2. EARTH POWER. "THE MACHINE"
Grounded, Producing Tangible Results.
Earth wants results and facts, practical solutions, grounded, disciplined action, tangible production, physical possessions, measurable quantities, realism and power. They are stable, controlled, ambitious, tenacious, analytical, plodding, rock solid, impersonal, rational, and into rules and perfectionism.
- **Taurus**: financier, contractor, designer-builder
- **Virgo**: the grind; healthy, workaholic, consultant
- **Capricorn**: an authority, executive leader, the boss

#3. AIR POWER. "THE THINKER"
Mental, Talker, Idea Person, People Person.
Air loves the mind and communication of ideas, mental abstractions, detached, objective, logical and rational thinking. They teach and share ideas and theories. Relationships and communications are essential. They are talkative, alert, articulate and social, the intellectual idea person.
- **Gemini**: the communicator & mental powers
- **Libra**: people person, partners, customers & competitor
- **Aquarius**: unique inventor, networking powers

#4: WATER POWER. "THE PSYCHIC"
Emotions, Feelings, Security & The Past
Water represents feelings and emotions, your personal psyche and your psychological connections with other humans, with the environment, and with the collective unconscious and spiritual world. They are compassionate, nurturing, intimate, cosmic, sensitive and creative.
- **Cancer**: the nurturing caretaker, vulnerable
- **Scorpio**: leveraged, transformer, power-broker
- **Pisces**: magician, shaman, the visionary

The Next 6 Profiles are *Combinations* of The Above 4 Profiles.

APPENDIX 4: BASIC ASTROLOGY

THE 10 PERSONALITY PROFILES for BUSINESS SUCCESS
Basic Styles of Decision-Making with
Your Business, Careers, Money & Investments

THE OTHER 6 PERSONALITY TYPES

These Next 6 Power Profiles are Combinations of Elements, When More Than One Element Is Strong;

#5: FIRE/EARTH POWER. "THE BULLDOZER"
The steamroller, earth mover and builder. They combine the fiery spirit and enthusiasm of fire with the dogged, determinism of earth, target their goal and produce results.
Aries, Leo and/or Sagittarius (Fire)
plus Taurus, Virgo and/or Capricorn (Earth)

#6: FIRE/AIR POWER. "THE SUPER-STAR"
The entertainer, cheerleader and champion of the masses. They're upbeat, fun-loving, inspiring and optimistic,; drawn to marketing, sales, politics, promotion, the stage and podium.
Aries, Leo and/or Sagittarius (Fire)
plus Gemini, Libra and/or Aquarius (Air)

#7: FIRE/WATER POWER. "THE PROMOTER"
The passionate, idealist advocate of causes and projects, especially in the media, entertainment and education. Like fire/air, but with a serious darkside and wide mood swings.
Aries, Leo and/or Sagittarius (Fire)
plus Cancer, Scorpio and/or Pisces (Water)

#8: EARTH/AIR POWER. "THE HUMAN COMPUTER"
The strategic planner, research analyst and problem-solver, they are effective, efficient, logical and grounded in practical realities. Organizational consulting with solid theoretical basis.
Taurus, Virgo and/or Capricorn (Earth)
plus Gemini, Libra and/or Aquarius (Air)

#9: EARTH/WATER POWER. "THE NURTURING SAVIOR"
The natural priest and shaman, the caretaker, nurturer and savior of the world. Serious, with a strong desire for personal security and a strong need to serve, help and heal people.
Taurus, Virgo and/or Capricorn (Earth)
plus Cancer, Scorpio and/or Pisces (Water)

#10: AIR/WATER POWER. "THE CREATIVE SPIRIT"
The creative genius, an idea generator, gifted with a great imagination, dreams, fantasies and archetypal stories, an inspired artist, writer, counselor, psychic, coach and teacher.
Gemini, Libra and/or Aquarius (Air)
plus Cancer, Scorpio and/or Pisces (Water)

WHEN COMBINING MORE THAN ONE PROFILE ... *if the mix of elements in your own chart indicates that you are strong in more than one of these combinations, then you should blend the two most important ones in interpreting your entrepreneurial strengths and orientation, or use the one that feels right to your inner astrologer.*

SIMPLIFIED "ZIP-CODE" INTERPRETATIONS for ASTROLOGY

The Same Zip-Code Number & Interpretation Applies to Each One ... the House, the Sign, AND the Planet with that Number. You can also use each one for either business or personal interpretations.

ZIP-CODE =	THE HOUSE =	THE SIGN =	THE PLANET
#1.	1st HOUSE	ARIES	MARS

personal: initiative, self, energetic, action, doing own thing
business: marketing identity, incorporation, shareholders

#2.	2nd HOUSE	TAURUS	VENUS

personal: earning power, grounded, values, finances, resources
business: earnings, financial budgets, investment strategies

#3.	3rd HOUSE	GEMINI	MERCURY

personal: mental reasoning, ideas, learning, conversational
business: communications, media, data, travel, education

#4.	4th HOUSE	CANCER	MOON

personal: family, home, foundations, roots, security, past history
business: real estate, plant & equipment, location, fixed assets

#5.	5th HOUSE	LEO	SUN

personal: creativity, charisma, risks, fun, coaching, loving, youth
business: management team, image, motivation, speculation

#6.	6th HOUSE	VIRGO	MERCURY

personal: service to others, health, work, critical, research
business: employee relations, health plans, inventories

#7.	7th HOUSE	LIBRA	VENUS

personal: all relationships, marriage, compete, cooperate, artist
business: partners, contracts, legal, competitors, diplomacy

#8.	8th HOUSE	SCORPIO	PLUTO

personal: intense power, in emotions, sexuality, money & spirit
business: leveraged resources, taxes, banking, insurance

#9.	9th HOUSE	SAGITTARIUS	JUPITER

personal: philosophy, idealism, optimism, self-discovery, travel
business: business mission, legislation, foreign markets, ethics

#10.	10th HOUSE	CAPRICORN	SATURN

personal: responsible, career, public power, authority, formal
business: leadership power, good will, national reputation

#11.	11th HOUSE	AQUARIUS	URANUS

personal: futurist, inventor, unique, goals, groups, networker
business: community network, political contacts, intangibles

#12.	12th HOUSE	PISCES	NEPTUNE

personal: behind scenes, compassion, illusion, psyche, spiritual
business: R&D, trade secrets, enemies, business intelligence

This concept of an astrological "Zip-Code" - a method of simplifying astrology by giving the same interpretation to a house, a sign and a planet - originated with Dr. Zipporah Dobyns, a psychologist and author of several books on the art and science of astrology. For an excellent summary of these Zip-Codes, see Pottenger's book, Complete Horoscope Interpretation.

About the Author

Paul Farrell first discovered the decision-making power of *Money Astrology* as a vice president with Morgan Stanley's real estate investment banking group where he worked on $1.5 billion of financing deals.

This new discovery occurred while attending a workshop on *Mythical Meditation* by Joseph Campbell, the author of *The Power of Myth* and the world's leading scholar on mythology. This unique opportunity opened him to J.P. Morgan's "secret" - the predictive power of astrology as a tool in making successful decisions in the business and financial world.

The concepts of the emerging new Money Astrology developed while Dr. Farrell was Executive Vice President and Chief Operating Officer of the Financial News Network, and later as Executive Vice President of Mercury Entertainment Corporation. His business and financial experience also includes vice presidencies with City Investing Company, Sonnenblick Goldman and the Property Development Group, as well as Associate Professor and Research Analyst at Cornell University and Associate Editor of the *Los Angeles Herald Examiner* newspaper.

Dr. Farrell received a Juris Doctor from the University of Virginia Law School, Masters of Regional Planning from Cornell University, Bachelors of Architecture from Carnegie Institute of Technology and a Doctorate in Clinical Psychology from the International College, where he completed a documentary on the male midlife crisis, "*Modern Man in Search of His Soul: Conversations with The Transforming Man.*" The Virgin Islands International Film Festival awarded him a gold medal for directing a short film, *Ophelia's Mascara,* and the Secretary of Defense gave him an award for photography. He has written and lectured about many subjects. He was featured in a *Venture* magazine cover story on "Rapid Learning Curves for Entrepreneurs."

www.ingramcontent.com/pod-product-compliance
Lightning Source LLC
Chambersburg PA
CBHW081014040426
42444CB00014B/3209